M000042838

CAPSULE
STORIES

Masthead

Natasha Lioe, Founder and Publisher
Carolina VonKampen, Publisher and Editor in Chief
April Bayer, Reader
Stephanie Coley, Reader
Rhea Dhanbhoora, Reader
Hannah Fortna, Reader
Kendra Nuttall, Reader
Rachel Skelton, Reader
Deanne Sleet, Reader
Claire Taylor, Reader

Cover art by Darius Serebrova
Book design by Carolina VonKampen

Paperback ISBN: 978-1-953958-08-2
Ebook ISBN: 978-1-953958-09-9

© Capsule Stories LLC 2021
All authors retain full rights to their work after publication.
No part of this book may be reproduced, scanned, distributed, or used in any manner without written permission of Capsule Stories except for use of quotations in a book review.

CAPSULE STORIES

STORIES

Autumn 2021 Edition

Contents

Letter from the Editors

Capsule Stories Autumn 2021 Edition begins with the poem "Reformation" by Rachel Bruce. She writes: "It is difficult to protect another season from ruin / at your hands. . . . You may have left me unsalvageable, / but I am determined to love my Octobers again." This poem captures an idea we wanted to explore in our Dancing with Ghosts theme: reflecting on memories and emotions tied to places, bodies, and seasons and figuring out how to move forward. Sometimes we rewrite those memories, reclaiming a place or season; sometimes we allow those memories to simmer, revisiting them again and again to find new meaning or purpose. We are continually making peace with our past, learning how our memories and experiences and people we loved have made us who we are today. As you read the stories, poems, and essays in this edition, we invite you to dance with your own ghosts, whatever they may be.

Dancing with Ghosts

There was a small cutout in the wall of a place you used to call home. You would sit in the hole, surrounded by walls and space, walls that were close together, space that felt limitless. Sometimes you would sit there and just think, let your mind wade through the distorted memories, seeing your life played back, rippling, as if you were underwater. Eating at the dinner table, engrossed by the sequel of a book you loved. Staring out into the small audience at your spelling bee, the absence of your parents weighing heavily. Sitting on the concrete with your back against the wall, silent, the noise of your classmates fading into the background, as the wind stirs a pile of dead leaves beside you.

You are a mosaic of the people who have let themselves into your life, of what they did to you, for you, around you. You let others make a home inside you to avoid feeling empty. You have always been more of a wallflower, waiting for things to happen to you, not feeling like you had the agency to make things happen for yourself. You might get the occasional rush of inspiration, the adrenaline propelling you to move forward. These are the moments that you want to be perceived by, but not the moments that you believe you are made of. These moments that pass through you, that happen to you—will you ever learn to grasp them before they dissolve?

Reformation

Rachel Bruce

Autumn casts its colors heavily into my eyes.
Reds and golds blend together in wet piles,
plastering the streets with orange;
it stains the soles of my shoes
and leaves a sour taste on the roof of my mouth.

It is difficult to protect another season from ruin
at your hands.
I burned all the orange in my house—
I remember how you used to wear it on your nails.

I crush leaf piles and imagine bones cracking.
You may have left me unsalvageable,
but I am determined to love my Octobers again.

Some Days Are Diamonds

Michael Colbert

Poofy dogs outnumber children. Air smells like cinnamon unless it smells like bear scat. Stetson hats emerge down the street, around the corner. Everything is of another world in Aspen. Yet we're here for more than alpine euphoria. My family came to Colorado to celebrate John Denver, gone twenty-two years.

As a kid, my mom thought John Denver would wait to marry her. Her enduring love of him scores my childhood. She would sing "Take Me Home, Country Roads" while washing dishes. My sisters and I warbled "Leaving on a Jet Plane" in the back of her Ford Taurus when summer vacation ended. Now, "Perhaps Love" always plays when she starts her car. Every time she picked up my grandmother from her assisted living unit for doctors appointments, for Thanksgiving or Christmas at our house, it would play. My mom tells me how my grandmother would say, "I listen to John Denver in your car," a memory, a new ritual for my grandmother to hold onto as her memories shuffled, a memory my mother now holds on to since my grandmother is three months gone.

Coming to Aspen, I grasp at the memories of a man my mother adored. His lyrics reside in place, and I want to inhabit this one, understand him and learn about her. The intensity of the landscape overwhelms my senses. Snow-striated mountains look like sugar-dusted crinkle cookies. Dark brown buildings in the Ashcroft ghost town splinter beneath swaths of yellow Aspen leaves. I've always sought strong connection to places, and maybe John Denver played some role in that for me. He composed stories from landscapes and their people. His lyrics appear on mountain vistas. In the John Denver Sanctuary, rocks assemble in an amphitheater before stones carved with his lyrics, a labyrinthine concert, a performance of mindfulness, a vigil.

Over the weekend, my mother tells us stories of her childhood with John. Some of these we've heard before. She saw him perform in Madison Square Garden and fanned a sign that said, "Far out." "Annie's Song" had my mom and her best friend in tears. John Denver wouldn't marry them. He had other loves.

We hike along the Rio Grande, on the hunt for the site of the *Rocky Mountain High* album cover. She tells me how she first came to John Denver with a 45 her brother didn't want and pawned onto her.

"I didn't realize he was giving me the album to get *rid* of it because he didn't like it. That didn't dawn on me until years later," she says. Golden aspens catch the light around us, concealing the Rio Grande below. We walk in twos, Mom and me in the back. "So first I listened to the album to gain acceptance from Jimmy, but then I came to love John purely for John, his beautiful, pure voice, his guitar playing, his love songs, his sadness, his expression through lyrics."

We find the spot, we think. Maybe the landscape has changed over the past fifty years. My sister wants to slide down, to stage the photo, but we're too afraid. My mom lights up at the view, a rock jutting over a waterfall.

She always indulged me as a kid—buying bracelets from my room sales, taking me out of school to attend writing events at the bookstore. Here, stories from her childhood condense. Her face glows when we all share this together, go to impersonator concerts, wander the sanctuary. I feel the joy of watching someone you love with her joy. Everything he has meant to her becomes embodied, is given a body, here. She and my father came here a year before for this celebration of John Denver, and so badly she wanted to share it with all of us.

Aspen is full of spirits. John in the tribute concerts, on the buttons the middle-aged pin to their shirts. My grandmother in the sanctuary, called forth by a song. When people speak of John, they say how much he had ahead of him, what the plane crash took, his environmental work, the legacy of his lyrics and voice.

I have a memory. My dad and sisters were out when my mom heard the news. John Denver had died in a plane crash. She folded into the living room couch, crying, and I found a spot beside her, just being there with her, a three-year-old observing his mother's grief. Though, this memory doesn't add up, the timing of it impossible based on when John Denver died, October 1997. We weren't even living in that house. Maybe it's not a memory, but a dream, a haunting I want to share with her.

My family has assembled here, together for the first time since my grandmother's funeral. She went fast, suddenly. None of us knew it was our last time seeing her. Eighty-seven, she told stories on the Fourth of July about her sister working for the Yankees and meeting Joe DiMaggio. In dreams, I hear her girlish laugh. I find myself searching for the citrus perfume she used to wear. My mom speaks of finding answers, learning what happened the night she went, why we never heard from the nursing home when she wasn't acting like herself. I can remember exactly how the call felt. My dad and I in a hotel room somewhere in Pennsylvania, moving me to North Carolina for school, the phone woke us past 1 a.m. I listened for my mom on the line with my dad. *My mom died.* None of us thought it could be real. It must be a prank, a dream.

Wandering the sanctuary, we find Denver's lyrics engraved on the rocks, and among them, this: "As it may be painful to lose contact with the physical aspect of one we love, the spirits can never be lost." My mother reads his words on a stone in the sanctuary. We inhale cinnamon air and feel the ghosts flutter Aspen leaves.

I've always sought strong connection to places

Imaging the Great Ancients

Xiaoly Li

A mountain of plum trees. That is where I meet
Lu You, poet of the defeated Song Dynasty.
He stops in front of every tree, whether
it blossoms or withered flowers fall. He walks
fast like a soldier brandishing a sword,
his strides too great to follow. I stop
on the hilltop, aim my camera toward him.
His figure appears everywhere.
Blossoming fragrance endures.

At the sea, I find Li Shangyin
under a huge late Tang Dynasty moon.
It beams of a thousand rays that kiss each wave.
He stands still, facing the moon.
I walk over quietly and sit on a rock.
Turning toward me, he flashes his eyes like pearls.
I wonder if they are warm tears and
wait for him to tell passing stories.

I can't drink, so I must wait until after
Li Bai, poet of the flourishing Tang Dynasty,
finishes three jugfuls of wine.
He raises his head, sighs, and holds the cup
toward the sky, laughing. He invites
the moon and his shadow to join him
in dance. His voice is mesmerizing.
I dance with him in the surrounding orchids and pines.

Tracks

Corinna Schulenburg

the leaves know
the tourists pay to see them
fade into fire
then fall
a dance of pendulums
down to the ghost-stained
earth.
crammed with her own
brace of voices
the girl traces
the way the sneakered boy
ran to the tracks,
not the track where he ran
from things
and where the band
crashed the football songs
while the brute boys
fell, no
the track where the train
would shudder
the ghost-stained earth
and call its name
in a whistle coming
a whistle going.
she stands there
like the sailor who set out
for gold
only to stumble
a lifetime later
upon home

stands there as the air brisks
her cheeks and chaps
her lips,
and then it happens:
she exhales the ghost
who is the sneakered boy
who is the whistle going
who is the leaves
falling straight
as knives
into
the living earth.

the ghost-stained earth

Bus Stop

Denise Nichole Andrews

i. when the bus stopped at the hill
    below our yellow country home
    grandfather was patiently waiting.

    in hand, a walking stick.
    at his side, our eight-year-old pup, ralph,
    panting in the september heat.

    all the children asked,
    who was that white man?
    why was he there for me?

    a little runt of a black girl
    with big hair and bigger glasses
    who missed her daddy.

    could it be an adoption?
    how were we related?
    preteens in the back of the bus,
    gossiping.

ii. we moved because of my mother
    because of her needs
    like wanting a dating pool of men
    who were not professional athletes.

    we moved because of my father
    because he wasn't fathering
    he wasn't calling
    he wasn't answering.

we moved for a new address,
a new job,
a new school,
a new harvest.

iii.   when grandfather and i
ran out of questions to ask,
we remained content
in the warmth of silence.

walking together
smiling sweetly
but i withheld
secrets that could
concern our family.

iv.   i never told him about the kids
on the bus who picked on me
or the fight with two girls
who made each other's scalps bleed.

while other kids egged them on,
i sank in my seat.

v.   a pack of wild dogs
sniffed through the bush.
tongues out,
teeth snarling.

alerting my grandfather
to our chickens' safety

---

those dogs must be starved to the point
where they could slip through the fence easily,
bite through the hens' necks,
we had to get them away from our property.

we walked faster
the pair of us plotting
how we could save the coop.

vi.   sometimes grandfather
would pick me up in a tractor
and let me steer

on those days
i felt as free as
a sixth grader could be

no fears
no lies
no secrets

just the land
and my grandfather
there to protect me.

719 Lombard

Carol Coven Grannick

I slipped back there
not in a dream of dimmed colors
but on a day of sun and scarlet maples
lit with neon-brushed orange
piles of leaves begging us
to crunch them with Keds.

Inside is the room not given, but grown:
twin desks with pull-down fronts
for poems and homework,
a dozen tiny cubbies
where treasures hide and wood smells
of pencils and pink erasers,
art gum crumbles stowed
alongside plastic gold and silver
gumball gifts bought with precious nickels,

a miniature moccasin,
an etched leather key case
a curled pink ribbon from an early birthday gift

placed on the end of our beds
as we slept, chiffon-like paper-wrapped
—often a book, a book of my own—

photos of ballerinas and horses
from newspapers, slick color magazines
taped up on wallpaper.

Then the summer
when it disappeared as if
insignificant shears the dream
and only the sister-shared bookshelf remains.

Gone, as if not mine.
Gone, as if outgrown.
Gone, as if unneeded,
un-longed for
un-remembered
for the dreams
they might have allowed
to come true

burned into the memory
left only for poetry
and the ancient smells of wood
and pencils and pink erasers
that seep from the words.

burned into
the memory
left only for poetry

Late Autumn Prairie Grass

Carol Coven Grannick

Do memories stay with you
as you leave your green of spring
and summer—

who trod here, whose fingers
ran through your strong, supple leaves,

what old woman touched you
like a bird's lost feather,
floating toward the browning earth?

Old Goliath

Emily Uduwana

There is a point in adolescence when most young girls embark on a kind of cycle. For many of my human friends, this involved hiding menstrual pads up their sleeves. For me, cycling meant learning to ride a bike. Specifically, learning to ride Old Goliath.

Old Goliath was an ancient mountain bike, barely holding it together after twenty-odd years traveling across the Pacific Northwest. With its adventuring years now behind it, it leaned rustily against the raised-bed gardens in our backyard, remaining upright only with the aid of Mom's resiliency charms. I spent my childhood perched on its seat, watching Mom sow sunflower seeds and unearth bright purple beetroots. Memories of Old Goliath mixed together with memories of my mother: the smell of her perfume, the scratchy wool of her sweaters, the leathery touch of her gardening gloves against my cheek.

I stopped spending time with Old Goliath when Mom passed away. Some things are too painful to hold on to—sometimes it's easier to forget them all at once.

My godmother, Judith, didn't think so. I'm sure you've heard that old adage about owners beginning to resemble their pets over time, fluffing up like standard poodles or turning droopy like ancient basset hounds. But Judith didn't age to resemble her hairless cat—a nasty old thing called Snuggles—or even the lizards that ran amuck behind her old folks' home. Instead, Judith steadily became more and more like an elephant. My godmother remembered *everything*, and she stored it all between her two enormous ears.

Two days after Mom died, Judith moved in to our little house near the woods. With a swish of her wand, she directed her train of boxes to settle themselves in the living room, guest bedroom, and basement. They slipped into place and began unpacking themselves without further ado. Judith, on the other hand, made a beeline for our attic, motioning for me to stay behind in the kitchen. With her perfect elephant-like memory, she'd remembered something important: a trunk she'd left behind years ago, stored away in the attic and seemingly forgotten. Except, of course, that my godmother never forgot anything.

Judith returned from the attic with a dusty old trunk and a smile brighter than the autumn sunlight streaming through the kitchen windows. She motioned for me to follow her to the table and then set the trunk down with a resounding *thud*. Another wave of her wand and the trunk flew open, its lid banging against the wooden tabletop. The trunk's contents rumbled like a hungry stomach, with such ferocity that both Judith and I flew back against the wall. Books of all shapes and sizes shot out of the trunk, zipping and soaring around the kitchen like great papery birds. The oldest and most dilapidated of the bunch toppled out of the trunk and onto the floor with a groan that sounded eerily human. It scooted slowly across the tiles, dragging its cover against the linoleum until it came to a stop at my feet. A grimoire.

My godmother surveyed the newly cluttered kitchen with a wide smile. "You, my dear," she declared smugly, "have some studying to do."

If Judith meant to distract me from my grief, she offered more than enough opportunities. My days—up to that point consumed with thoughts of my mother—became a series of back-to-back magic lessons. Mirroring the kitchen, my bedroom floor turned into a miniature maze of grimoires. And, in truth, the entire house became an enchanted hazard zone: flying plates, self-lighting hearths, and talking wallpaper transformed our day-to-day lives. Judith filled my after-school hours with charms demonstrations, potion making, and defensive maneuvers. I learned quickly that my godmother could turn just about anything into a magical how-to-do, from baking cookies to banishing wasps from the garden.

Then, one afternoon, when I'd gone almost two hours without thinking of my mother, Judith pulled the flying carpet out from under me. Setting her mug of spiced tea onto the coffee table, she leaned forward to place a hand on my knee.

"You know," she began gently, "your mother wrote her own grimoire when she was your age." She flicked a finger into the air, and a spiral-bound notebook appeared in my lap. Mom's spell book was nothing like the ancient leather tomes from Judith's trunk. Looped writing and scribbled hearts dominated its shiny purple cover, left behind by glitter pens and permanent marker. Left behind by my mother.

I flipped the notebook open to find spells scrawled in the margins of every page: recipes for acne and body hair removal, step-by-step instructions for mixing love potions, and there—on page sixty-five—the words to Old Goliath's resiliency charm. In the weeks since Judith had moved in, I'd nearly forgotten about the old bike, rusting away out back.

"I want to learn this one," I decided aloud. I held the notebook out to Judith, pointing to the resiliency charm. Written in cursive under a section on enchanted jump ropes, the spell included a twenty-year-old doodle of Old Goliath.

"An interesting choice." Judith raised a penciled-in eyebrow at me, crossing her heavily bangled arms across her chest. "You're twelve years old, dear. What could you possibly need a resiliency charm for? Your aching back?"

I scowled at her, sinking into the chair across from hers. I ran my fingers along a gouge in the coffee table, left behind by one of Mom's enchanted knitting needles.

"I just want to learn it, okay?"

"Well, alright then," Judith said simply. I lifted my head suspiciously, surprised by the sudden capitulation. Her eyes sparkled as they blinked back at me from behind half-moon spectacles. She held Mom's spell book in her lap, one of her fingers absentmindedly tracing the doodle of Old Goliath.

"That's it?" I asked hesitantly.

"That's it." Judith closed the grimoire and set it on the coffee table. Dusting her hands off on her long paisley apron, she stood and motioned for me to join her in the garden. "Best not to start with human trials. If I remember correctly, your mom used to practice these kinds of charms on my old mountain bike."

I started, nearly falling off my chair. "Old Goliath was *your* bike?"

"One and the same."

I stared at my godmother as she crossed the living room to the back door and jammed her big feet into even bigger Wellies.

She looked up at me impatiently. "Are you coming or what?"

I nodded, watching as my godmother slipped into the garden.

My godmother's old bike.

I'd always assumed Old Goliath was Mom's. She'd told me so many stories about her travels across Oregon and Washington, how she'd zoomed past giant redwood trees and enchanted the bike to fly on cloudy days.

Picturing crotchety, elephant-eared Judith on that bike was a whole lot harder. Even in Mom's old photo albums, my godmother always had little gold-rimmed glasses and big, poofy white hair. I couldn't remember *ever* having seen her without her signature flowing dresses and worn-out aprons. What had she been like at my age, swapping stories and magic spells with my Grandma Clarisse?

Shaking the questions from my head, I grabbed my mother's spell book from the coffee table and followed Judith into the garden. I shivered as I stepped onto a bed of cold grass, the day's chill seeping into my bones.

"There you are." Judith waved me over to where she stood between two raised-bed gardens. Old Goliath leaned pitifully against one of the cobwebbed wooden walls, its handlebars rusted and its paint job peeling from the recent rains. The ancient bike seemed even older than I'd remembered. I stared down at its deflated tires, feeling as run-down as Old Goliath looked.

My godmother's authoritative voice broke through my thoughts.

"Now, your mother wrote a lot of spells in her time," Judith said, motioning for me to come closer. "But this one requires a particular kind of strength. You have to be the boss of this bike. Got it?"

I nodded, even though I very much did *not* get it.

"Old Goliath here has been chugging along since I was a girl—so that's, hmmm, let's not put a number on that one, actually. Let's just say, this old boy's got some years under its belt drive."

Judith patted the worn leather seat. "Hop on then," she ordered.

I balked, pressing my back against the door to the greenhouse. "Why?"

I wanted to *restore* the bike—not ride it.

Judith only frowned, pushing up her glasses with one hand. "How else will you know what needs fixing, dear? The best way to find weak points in a bike is to ride it."

"No."

Sudden tears pricked the backs of my eyes, hot and sharp. *Why had I picked this spell?*

Of course Judith would expect me to ride the darn thing. What would she think of me when she knew the truth, that I'd never bothered to learn how to ride the bike Mom loved so much? The bike *Judith* loved so much?

"No," I said again, more firmly this time. I scowled up at my godmother, ignoring the guilt that pricked at my insides. Judith scowled right back.

But her face softened almost immediately as she took in my clenched fists and trembling lower lip. "Oh," she said softly, her eyes becoming a bit misty. "Oh dear."

I frowned, swiping at the moisture in my eyes.

"Mom was going to teach me," I muttered defensively, even though Judith hadn't asked. "She said I could learn whenever I wanted. I was going to—I *would* have learned—"

But Old Goliath had always seemed so rickety and rusted, as if it could fall apart at any moment. And, anyway, I had been so comfortable sitting on its seat in the garden, leaning safely against the warm wooden walls as Mom weeded beside me.

But now Mom was gone and there was nothing warm about anything.

Judith's voice broke through my thoughts.

"Let's take the day off," she suggested gently. I looked up to see her smiling at me from beside Old Goliath, her arm wrapped around its body as if it, too, was a beloved godchild. "There's more to life than the rote memorization of spells. Go change into some proper shoes and a good thick sweater while I fix up Old Goliath's dangerous bits. I'll meet you by the front door."

More to life than memorizing spells. I side-eyed my godmother from the passenger seat as we drove to a forest near the edge of the town, dubious of her sincerity.

But she repeated those words again as she stood at the mouth of a bike path, one hand placed obstinately on each hip. "There's more to life than learning magic," she said firmly. "*You* won't be using any today."

"What?" I gaped at her in disbelief. "Why not?"

Judith raised an eyebrow at me. "You're not the only witch around, you know. And besides, you need to learn this properly. Off you go."

Old Goliath stood between us, its metal body wavering slightly in the cold breeze. To be fair, it looked less rickety than I'd ever seen it, the wheels and handlebars shining with new life from Judith's spellcasting. Still, I figured it wouldn't make much difference how pretty the bike was if I was staring up at it from the ground.

"What about a protection spell?" I bargained, peering hopefully up at Judith. Just because *I* couldn't practice magic didn't mean *she* couldn't help me out. And like she'd said—I wasn't the only witch around. My godmother answered by dumping a helmet into my arms.

"There's your protection spell," she said firmly. "Now get going. I'll send something along to help you in a bit."

I scowled at her, but I grabbed Old Goliath by the handlebars and dragged it down the bike path. Admittedly, Judith had picked a pretty area for me to wipe out in. The path was lined with giant redwoods and smaller pine trees, and the air smelled deliciously like fall. I wondered how badly I'd have to injure myself for Judith to brew up her famous cinnamon apple cider.

I walked about a half-mile down the path, wondering how far I was supposed to go. The forest grew progressively darker as I rolled Old Goliath along, the canopy thickening overhead with whispering green needles.

Then there was a bang and a flash and, a few feet in front of me, an image of my godmother puffed into existence. Except I could tell from the flickering of her body and the smoothness of her skin that this was not the Judith I knew. Beside her, a pretty redheaded woman stood with her arm around a child's shoulders. *Grandma Clarisse.*

I leaned cautiously against Old Goliath as the memory spell played out down the road. Judith—younger despite her puffy white hair and glasses—dragged a reluctant little girl away from my grandmother and down the tree-lined path before me. The two of them waved goodbye to Grandma Clarisse, who faded into the blurry edges of the memory. My chest tightened as I recognized the child trailing after Judith. It was my mother, five years old and scowling something fierce behind a cloud of curly red hair.

"But I don't *want* to ride that bike!" she snapped at Judith, tugging her little arm free. "I want the *pink* one from the *store!*"

"Well, this is the one you have," Judith said cheerfully. Old Goliath came into view ahead of them, its shiny blue body sparkling metallic in the sun. Distracted for a moment from the memory spell, I glanced down at the worn-out bike by my side, sitting dully under the chilly autumn sky. There was nothing shiny about it anymore.

When I looked back up, the younger, cheerier version of Judith had deposited my mother onto Old Goliath's seat. She plopped a familiar blue helmet onto her head, and it fell immediately over Mom's face, covering her eyes and bopping her on the nose. Mirroring them, I buckled the same helmet into place on my own head.

In the memory, Judith chuckled warmly. She performed a quick resizing spell while Mom squirmed, the helmet still covering her eyes and nose.

"Take a deep breath," young Judith said firmly. Her holographic figure turned toward me with an expectant expression, and I was pulled back to reality with a jolt.

I sucked in a shaky gulp of air. The fuzzy image of Judith nodded smugly, as if she could see me following her instructions.

"Good," she said, turning back to my mother. "Now it's your turn, Ella."

"I don't know who you're talking to," Mom responded sourly. But she took in a noisy breath anyway and waited for further instructions.

Judith walked us both through the motions of riding Old Goliath. Together with my five-year-old mother, I learned to balance my feet on its pedals and bike wobbly circles around the memory spell.

After a short lesson, Mom grew bored of Judith's instructions.

"I'm ready!" she insisted, leaning eagerly over the handlebars. "Can I go, or what?"

My godmother laughed, a deep, throaty sound I hadn't heard since before Mom died. She waved an arm at my mother. "Go!"

Mom set off at a rapid pace, pedaling furiously down the path. I hurried to orient myself on Old Goliath and then dashed off after her.

We biked side-by-side down the rocky dirt road, our faces

flushing in unison and our wild red hair flying along behind us. After a while, my heart stopped seizing at the sight of each rock and tree in our path. I relaxed against Old Goliath, my feet finding a reliable pattern on the pedals, the crisp autumn air finding the slopes and valleys of my face. It was a calm I hadn't felt in months. Watching this fierce, childhood version of my mom zigzag down the trail made me feel almost as if we were together in the garden again. I could almost smell the leather of her gloves, the warm soil as she patted it into place, the saltiness of her sweat. The smell of *her*.

But after a time, the flickering mirage of Judith's memory began to fade. My mother faded along with it, the image of her shifting and shimmering until I was alone again in the forest. The path we'd followed between redwood trees and sweet-smelling pines suddenly felt incredibly isolated. Still, something within me wanted to go on. With my feet still finding a rhythm against Old Goliath's pedals, I closed my eyes and inhaled the scent of the forest.

It was my first deep breath in a long time.

The snap and flash of a camera startled me out of my reverie. I opened my eyes to see Judith—older but just as white-haired—waving wildly from a few yards away. She stood at the mouth of the forest with an old Polaroid camera in one hand. She grinned at me, and I grinned back, letting a gust of wind fill my lungs.

When I finally came to a stop and slipped off Old Goliath, Judith handed me the Polaroid she had taken. I watched as it developed in the palm of my hand, the image flickering slowly into view.

A girl with flushed cheeks flew down a tree-lined path, grinning as her red hair billowed out behind her. I stared

---

down at the photograph for a long moment before realizing the girl was me.

"You look just like your mother here," Judith whispered, her voice catching.

We stared down at the photograph together, sharing the same memory. A long moment went by before a brisk wind enveloped us, disturbing the fallen leaves at our feet and sending a chill through the air. A few more minutes passed before we felt up to moving. But when we did, we led Old Goliath back to the car together, each of us holding tight to one rusted blue handlebar.

The Yellow House at Tumnus Woods

Bethany F. Brengan

Old friends divulge
that there's an ugly metal fence
now collaring the property. My mother doesn't
want to know. But I would like to see it, once.
I spent years reading in the low-
branched maple, or whispering to my journal
behind the ancient barbershop turned
woodworking shed, or rolling marbles
in the grout grooves between
kitchen tiles, or racing up and down the stairwell,
the scenery of my mother's mural flashing past.
I stitched together stories
about a water nymph in the backwood
pond and dryads along the barely
trickling creek. I invested summers in drawing
maps, dividing the yard into enchanted
kingdoms. If I go back and the magic

is gone, it only means
we took it with us.

Fall Pears

Bethany F. Brengan

I. Late August

My predecessors were late Irish
and German immigrants, shuffling
after the thin trail of money:
railroads and factories and education. Farming
speaks of swampland in County Armagh
and the ill fit of rural Russia to unorthodox girls—
land soon abandoned, unlamented.

I have folded over recipes
in stomach-tensing hope—pears
with sweet potatoes, pears baked
with walnuts, pear salad, pear and chicken
stir-fry—caressing the too-green grit
between my lip and lower gum.
This is the season of wait.

I believe, as if there were no steel, no books,
no nuclear plants, everything depends on this:
Lord willing, the pears will come in.

II. Early September

This time last year you came (no regrets—
you told me after), but I don't remember the pears.
Were there pears that year?

The bees are disappearing.
There are not plenty of fish,
and soon there will be too much sea.
Our own fault too
(all cards on the table, I said,
I'm no good at games),
but I wish you could see
how I can cast this net into the sky
and pull back abundance. The pears
bleed white where this brash orange
basket on a pole breaks
their shape, and I taste sweet. A black fly
with red eyes skims the air and, pretending
to be a trickle of sweat, lands on my forearm.
I laugh and cast again. I will feed a city.

(Was this in the picture of the woman
you carried to meet me?
Some nights, I dream I am her.)
Confession: this is a tree
some stranger planted.

III. Now

We are making pear sauce
in my mother's kitchen when the wind
moves Midwest. We cannot watch the news;
we do not know that a rare trick of nature,
exciting to local meteorologists,
gives us hurricane forces far inland.
We do not even know that camera crews
are still struggling to find the heart

of the nothing below us. But we realize
we are the lucky ones. (I'm sorry I am happy
without you.)

There was more wind
than wet. The neighbor's corn is drunk
in the field and still too dry.
Our yard is a battlefield of bees,
wasps, and red-eyed flies, draining
the yellow grenades we couldn't reach,
didn't need. Too much for us,
but not enough to send a jar to everyone we love.
(Do you know you are the good man
my friends cannot find? One hundred years

ago, I would have been
a fool to send you home.) I was never the child
who, asked to bless the bounty, played pious,
then cried out a sacred, one-word pun.
(I want you to be as content
as I am this instant.) But now I whisper
that one prayer continuously,
reaching across the checkered cloth,
hands, in this moment, full.

The Ghost

Bethany F. Brengan

It's time
to give her up, the woman
you thought you were going to be
by this stage of life—
the way you release
the painting in your mind halfway
through picking up the brush.
Her silver sketch
enchanted your sad hours,
but no one kisses her canvas,
presses thumbs between her
thick, crooked whorls of color.
I won't say she isn't real,
or loved, but it's the living now
that needs affection.
And you are here, beautiful,
and not yet at rest.

I Keep This Pocket of Pain

Kalisse L. Van Dellen

Rebecca, my therapist of four years, doesn't know
I'm infertile. I don't know why I never told her.

Maybe it wasn't painful enough at the beginning, and then
it was too painful, and now it's been too long to bring it up.

(Like my neighbor who thinks I'm from Montana, and I don't
know how to correct him, so we talk about fishing and guns.)

Rebecca, my therapist, knows damn near everything
else about me: shuddered childhood, incessant rage, sex life,

every job I've scraped myself to earn, and my constant fear
that a cosmic shoe will drop again and I'm the only constant.

Rebecca, my therapist, tells me to enjoy my evenings
my daily void from 5:30 until midnight

because I'll be so much busier after I have kids
and I've worked so hard, I should find a hobby, just for me.

But I am Hypatia in eternity.
How am I supposed to
enjoy something
that I know will never
end?

Hourglass House

Nora Boyle

the gargoyles perched by the sunroof
pelt oversized grains of sand
at my head and i am wading
through debris
in my hourglass house

my limbs are heavy
hauling around imaginary armfuls
of broken china dolls
eyes loll from their sockets
unstitched locks wilt from their scalps
i spend days trying to plaster and sew
my imaginary friends back together
but their scars are vivid and horrific
and i hide them in the bathtub
then draw the curtain
i stare into the mirror
at my own unblinking eyes

i think *Sleeping Beauty* must be told backward . . .
as a child, she was always my favorite
i liked how she lived in the woods with fairies
and how her dress got to be both pink and blue
no one told me Sleeping Beauty had been raped
and that someday i too would sleep for a hundred years
i think the story must be told backward
that the sleep came after the prince, not before

i am wading through my hourglass house
with a dull persistent headache
losing friends like dead skin cells
and drinking old coffee
my arms cradling imaginary broken girls
i cannot put back together
i curl into bed
brush away the sand
gathering in my tear ducts
and wait for an ending
that may never come

wait for an ending

that may never come

Legacies

Nora Boyle

i've given birth to myself so many times
i'm surprised i'm still elastic
i picture myself full of blinking eyes
clinging to my fallopian tubes
in erratic constellations
i fall asleep counting them
like a child counts sheep
i'm not sure if this makes me more or less anxious
but regardless, it is exhausting
i wake up with more sleep
and fewer bags under my eyes
my body is happy but my brain is . . .
there are some poems i refuse to write
because they would be too painful to read
i am not a perfect daughter
but i am good at keeping secrets

Heavy

Maggie Bowyer

I've forgotten how to daydream;
These days my mind is constantly
Wondering why my ankles
Won't stop cracking or why
My chest has become so tight,
If it's worth the fight with doctors
Who might just say it's in my head—
Another reason for those I love
To continue to disbelieve me
When it comes down to
All the assistance, understanding
And persistence I might need.
These silences used to mean time
Spent in my mind palace, traversing
A land full of sugar gliders and
Friends made of the wind—
These pauses in between reality
Used to feed my creativity.
Now all my mental space is taken
Up by a pile of medical bills in
Disarray, diagnoses I am unsure
How to explain away, push into
The darkest corners of my brain
Where I can cover them up
With tattered sheets, shame
Blanketing my abilities, or
Lack thereof. These days my mind

Is as fried as the tender skin
Of my abdomen, covered in scars
Created by constantly crushing
Heat into the dried and strung out
Pain-stricken organs beneath.
These days it has become an
Impossible feat to stare out
A window, at ease. These days
There are daggers in my feet
Even as I am resting. These days
There is not a moment of rest,
A second of daydreams, a moment
Of reprieve from this body.

I've forgotten how
to daydream

What Lives Beneath the Buried

Kara Knickerbocker

Gullkistan Residency, Iceland

"17,000 earthquakes hit Iceland in the past week. An eruption could be imminent." —*CNN**

I'm sitting alone at the kitchen table when I first feel the shake, so sudden and strange that I stay still, stunned, for what feels like a thousand seconds just to make sure the balance was still in my head, the breath still in my body. I text the other residents to see if they felt anything in the next house over. They haven't. But shortly after, the news reports confirm I am not crazy. The fault lines form headlines—the Richter scale measuring it at 5.7. Though it's miles away from the village where my cabin is nestled, I have just felt my first earthquake.

I came here because I needed a shift. I wanted the space and time to write, which was the only way I knew of understanding where I stood, the only way I could think of how to move Earth. Maybe it's always been there, but the past few years, I felt pressure building. The breakup, the diagnosis, something red still burning through me, on the urge of breaking open. The taste of ash like a foreshadow on my tongue. The fissures already ran deep, but now there was the weight of more added layers: the upheaval of a new world with a spreading virus, the end of an apartment lease, the layoff from my job. Moving back to my hometown and back in with my parents. Planes and people were grounded, but I was in air, more suspended than ever. These weren't the changes I could have predicted—it was like none of the maps for all my big plans drawn to scale.

With excitement deepening, I read updates about the shakes. Luckily no nearby towns seem to be in danger's reach, but the rumbles still continue, and the scientists keep watch. It's like all of Iceland has their eyes open. There is a camera pointed in the direction of Keilir, waiting and ready, should an eruption occur. I check it every now and then from my open laptop, unable to form thoughts into writing of any magnitude. Or maybe I'm avoiding it. The chair here in the studio reminds me of my last therapist's office, back in Pittsburgh. The same welcoming colors, same plushness, but a seat you struggled to sit up straight in, a place you never felt you could be completely comfortable. I think about chairs I've sat in waiting for answers, the labels printed neatly on the medication, how I cycled through so many of both. How nice it has been to not need to remember to take a pill every morning, and in the next breath, wonder if I should. But the prescriptions have long expired—the only bottle I've never finished. The pills sink down into the bottom of a trash bin.

I imagine myself then as the mountain. My family, the doctors, my friends, all with their own lens carefully angled at my life. Monitoring the activity, trying to understand what was bubbling underneath, waiting for the explosion.

In the third decade of my life, I still didn't know the tremors of my own body. They happened when I had already lost consciousness. The fainting first happened when I was in high school, but all the tests came back inconclusive. An old flame told me once, after seeing it happen, how my arms locked up, my wild eyes retreated, the jerk of my legs until everything went limp on the bathroom floor. Turns out there were no seismic waves, no current sending signals to the heart or the brain. The next time it happens, I lie dormant in a hospital bed, hooked up to a machine. With thirty seconds of a heartbeat stopped, I am as close to extinct as one can get.

As I walk near the lake's edge, it is hard to imagine any friction here. The water is still as a silk sheet, not even the usual two ducks gliding over top its smooth bed. Fog cradles the base of the mountain, a gentle embrace of morning. Nothing is red, imminent. It is gray, but in a way that is quiet, healing. I walk the same footpaths through Laugarvatn as I have for the past month, wondering how I lived not knowing them before. I start writing more and more poems about bright blue and birds, and less about blood red and burning.

After the surgery, my chest grows its own small mountain: a foreign device pushed against skin. About one million people a year worldwide are implanted with a pacemaker. I just never thought I'd be one of them. The line where they have sliced into my body leaves a hot red crack, settles with stitches, softening to faint pink with time. I touch the landscape of my body, feeling like a stranger every time.

Volcanoes can produce rich, fertile land. Even with the aftershock that comes months after, as rocked as I am by the truth of his choice, I do not question my own. I have never felt the pull toward motherhood. Unlike the 0–9 of the Richter scale, there can be no range in which my *no* colors into his *yes.* And because of this, there is no future that we will touch like that again. Despite the hurt that splits through my center, I do not break. I chase the boundaries of other countries, forgetting about the only one we ever visited together.

Sometime over the last couple years, red spots have popped up on the bare map of my body. I pick them open, little globes of blood pooling from the wound. I pick at first to feel control, but then I cannot stop. I pick until scars spread out like a volcanic system. I am a danger to myself.

When I looked for writing residencies online, I didn't expect to choose one in Iceland. Especially not during a pandemic when international travel wasn't feasible. But the email came back with an acceptance. The timing of my life was right, and I couldn't deny the force. I could already feel all the words rising in my throat. I wondered what it would be like to come to the place where we took our anniversary trip. If memories would waterfall back, or if I'd feel a change at all.

The curse of Iceland's weather is that it is unpredictable, at best. The blessing is that you must wear layers. Covered in thermals and wool sweaters, my warm clothing becomes a shield from my own two hands. With less of my bare skin visible to examine and dig at imperfections, it begins to heal.

"Alda said there hasn't been an eruption there since the Ice Age!" I tell my mother, who is almost three thousand miles away, looking at the news from her own cabin back in Pennsylvania. Her worry is thick through the phone, until I loosen it with reason. She doesn't ask if I've applied to jobs, or met any "nice men" yet, just says, "You always did like adventure," and that she loves and misses me. It is still in the midst of an Icelandic winter, but already I feel the cold in me melting. Setting the table with one plate, I pull out the frozen parts of me I've deemed unworthy, letting them thaw in the kitchen. Later, in bed, my stomach stretched with food,

I cradle my palm over my heart. No longer strangers, we rise and fall that way together into the basalt of night, into sleep.

The news updates are slowing now, but I've already understood what I need to. I turn off the livestream of Keilir, let nature do her own powerful thing. I focus back to the blank page before me, black letters like ash beginning to rain slowly down in place and think, *all in our own beautiful time.*

*https://edition.cnn.com/2021/03/03/world/iceland-volcano-eruption-keilir-intl-latam/index.html

Surface

Cassie McDaniel

---

for Billie

Across the field of corn rows that look as though they point,
but lead to nowhere, I throw an empty idea against the scene
but can't make out the edges, my body without space
or weight, unable to articulate the thought much less contort
the memory of something there once was, or was coming.

In the car, around the twists and bends in the road
through new developments, the sky is trying.
Alight with pinks and purples, fiery and dropping,
I lose myself in it, the way a person gets lost in Walmart,
giving over to an identity that is not mine.

The house is quiet and dirty. I like it quiet. He runs his thumb
along the counter's edge. Neighbors and acquaintances
get touched on shoulders and hands.
He speculates about their lives. My answers to his questions
are long and vague. He delights in other people laughing.

On the floor I cross my legs, my skin pulling from bones
as if retreating, a puddle of wrinkles stretching and folding.
I am a corn field, or a long road, gliding along the surface
as an inconsequential breeze.

Tiny whimpers. We are alone.
She roots my nipple in the night, her wet mouth warm,
a soft and furry head against my arm. I settle,
until I'm not connected anymore. An unroped boat,
an undelivered letter, and still my girl, I hold her.

Leaf Falling

Betty Doyle

We sit in the car outside the pharmacy,
again, waiting for the doors to open.
Early morning, mid-October:
Sunday's drowsy quiet,
and the shop shutters glittering
in the not-quite-yet-frost.

The doctor will not let you
into the small room with me.
You must stay in your seat
opposite the shelf that stacks
lube, tampons, home HIV tests,
and pregnancy kits
all next to each other.

You must listen from beyond
the burnished brown door,
the same color as the leaves
that have fallen and gleaned,
turned to muck in the gutters.
Autumn's blooming ember shades,

now stewed and shrunk down
to a dying brown,
like roadside drifts of dirty snow.
There are no birds in these few trees,
bare behind the window and piercing
this morning's unkind sky.

You must listen when I am asked
when was the last day of your last cycle
and I try to picture
what the moon was doing that day,
whether she was pregnant with light
or rolling blind;

what we were doing
what we did last night
when we didn't think, only felt,
only needed something deep from each other,
and how afterward we watched
early fireworks from your bright window,
holding hands.

only needed something deep
from each other

August

Betty Doyle

Late summer is perfecting her menu
of allergies and melancholy.
Yesterday I saw a swarm of butterflies
nesting in the buddleia,
its rich magenta sun-whitened to dull lilac;
and I thought—you should be a year old,
beginning to roll these nouns around
on a small tongue that I grew,
uncertain at first, surprised by your discovery.
I think about this a lot,
how your lips would part and round,
all jaw and nose, vocal cords and lungs.
How those lips were never stained deep bloody purple
from the plump of roadside blackberries.
How blood looks so bright
against white porcelain, white cotton—
imprinted, and slightly cracked, like a dry kiss.

Halloween
1991

Sheleen McElhinney

I wear a paper-mache head
cupped over my human head.
A lumpy globe molded
by the hands of my mother.
My older siblings a flurry
of chatter and flammable
fabric just within earshot.
I am top-heavy but no one
can see my blonde curls, my big
stupid doe eyes. I am alone
with my breath, the muffled
swoosh of a heartbeat in my ears
like I'm back in the womb,
which is the next best thing
to being dead. I can say
whatever I want and no one
will hear me. Like *I think
there's something wrong with me.*
Or *I don't like myself.*
I can't see out of the finger poked
holes, too high above my vision.
I lift my small hand to paw
at the dark and hope that someone
will take it.

Witches of
Westbrook

Sheleen McElhinney

I watched my sisters,
    each of them trailing familiar scents
        like oil of Olay, eucalyptus,
  like brushfire, like smoke.
      Watched the pale moonstone glow
    of their skin brown in another year
of sun, and another. Watched their love
    turn into swollen bellies, their arms turn
        into cradles. Watched the corners
  of their eyes grow lines like the pages
of an open book. Watched them hurl
      fruit at husbands leaving, whip their hair
  in defiance. I watched them lift their wet
faces to the next approaching storm, slip
    into new armor as unassuming as gossamer.
      I was so much younger. Their long, lean bodies
      had stopped growing by the time
        I was born. They had already known
      the loss of a brother, gone
    before I arrived. Their small, smooth
fingers tracing the blue satin lining
of his new lidded bed. Their hands opening
and closing his tin box of trinkets,
  matchbox cars rusting in the salt from their
    eyes. They had felt the sprawling distance
      between the door and their father
        walking out, our mother tied to the bed
      to save her from herself, only waking
    for another heavy dose to take her back
  under, while they toiled, stared into an empty
pantry, learned to use the stove.

I still had a brother to love, then lose, my own
    hand to rest upon a frozen chest in the stillness
        of a quiet room. I still had children to birth, men
            to warm me then leave me
                cold, my own heart crushed like a fig.
    I watched my sisters because I wanted to learn
    how to slip like a sandcastle into the sea,
        or dissolve like a snowflake on the tongue.

*the stillness
of a quiet room*

Later Shades of Girlhood

Sheila Mulrooney

For my mother

I. When he and I left at the evening's call,
    how could I know you'd think to wait? The dawn
    still hours off, the August bugs awake.
    There's only one blue moon in summertime,

    he said, and asked to catch its rippling gold
    off of the lake. So hand in hand we went,
    forgiven by the gathering dusk and warmth
    of things untold. I didn't think of you

    when in the whispered rushes of first love,
    I let the water take those promises
    that only youth will give. New life entwined.
    A simple knot. Why would I hesitate?

    To find you in your wicker chair, watching
    for my return—the night had grown so late—

II. What is it like to fall in love, I'll ask.
    Together you and I are wandering through
    that predawn hour when night empties itself
    for mothers and their daughters, sleepwalkers.

    You'll say that once your mother left Ukraine
    she only spoke of love in the old world.
    These swamps, their swollen bugs, they left no room
    untouched. The humid air warping her bones

until the final shades of girlhood cracked,
splintered, then calloused in her sleep. Softness
does not exist for those estranged from home.
Our walks will end under the lightening sky,

as if our footsteps slowly woke the earth.
We rose to close the shutters in reply.

III.   The birds won't sing at twelve o'clock, you say.
They fear the looming noon, a moment's loss
of shadowed things. I never could explain
what silence meant, but would not trade the gift

of waking as a girl to see you perched
on our front porch, listening for morning's end.
I grew to think of you as a season
who would not shift until the autumn when

I packed my bags to go with him, then left.
How could I know that was the day you'd rise
to meet the arching sun and tell the birds
that they were safe? Your calls, *come out, come back,*

met with the hush of rustled wings and gold
sunbeams which fell straight down. Nothing was black.

I grew to think of you
as a season

On Renting an Airbnb in Wellsville, New York

Sheila Mulrooney

You go to the cottage because the cottage could be
anything. Faded white brick, faded blue paint,
rooms your feet want to own. Your speech swirls
in large quiet. You know there are ghosts here.

The cottage could be anything and the ghosts could be
anyone, except that they couldn't. Green cushions on
wooden chairs; velvet pillows on rocking chairs:
empty and pregnant, pregnant with absence.
You sit on the carpet, next to an elderly stain;
your blood flows cold at the chairs' angles,
angled toward each other. They've been talking
this whole time. Silent words, words not yours.

You go to the cottage because, for the first time,
you have a ghost of your own and you need to kill her.
Her eyes between your skull and skin; her mouth between
your world and ear. You ought to know her by now
but knowing her would give you something,
would make you something. That's why you go
to the cottage, because the cottage could be anything,
is nothing, could help you choke your ghost.

But the cottage has its own ghosts, faded into the carpet,
the chairs, the bricks. You hear their silence laugh at you;
you hear your ghost join in: *Not anything, not nothing,*
all of this is something, something. Something which
cannot be yours, someone whom you cannot kill,
quiet that's not yours to break.

Rite of Committal

JR Starzynski

I invited you to the funeral with a gilt-edged paper grail
that unfolded like origami into serifed sepia calligraphy.
You never sent your RSVP, but I received it by telepathy:
I was always too much. Like the treasure map you lost—
forgotten silver forks buried, tarnished, bent under rock.
I cried for what I'd found in your eyes: apocryphal gospel
floating in a bottle, model ship braving the vast Atlantic,
sailing on a prayer. I was free, once it sunk, to mourn
the better man I'd been when I'd held your hand.
Now a snuffing pool of wax checks the candle's glow.
The modern grotto is a church basement with cold cuts
on a folding table set up on fresh-scrubbed linoleum tile.
I slipped Father Tom a twenty to say a second homily
just for me while we stared into the yawning grave.
Yellow maple leaves blanketed the dark gray clay.
There weren't enough orchids in the world to satisfy
my sorrow or weigh down the past so it would stay
where no one else would see. He knew some of our story,
only the parts I shared begrudgingly in the confessional.
Holy Ghost, I atoned enough for those, hand clutching
the back of the pew in front of me. I said the entire rosary.
It was a heavy chain. This time he spoke of the light yoke,
the good shepherd, the virgins with their oil, and patience.
When we touch on innocence, no one mentions the man,
as if only women have something luminous to lose, as if love
is something taken, something ruined, not something shared,
like bread—though even bread, they said, should be broken
before it is consumed. What I would give to not relive
these memories of you, but love is a set of arms wide open,
a kiss on the cheek to please the Roman soldiers and when
it's over, someone always says no: No, I never knew him.

The Guest

JR Starzynski

I let you in because I thought you'd stay.
I couldn't make you make yourself at home.
Hospitality has no such expectations.
Yet when I turn, I still expect you there.
Must be my bad manners. The doorbell chimes
and I answer it, but it's just myself, casting bricks
at my front door like some grand romantic gesture
misremembered. Your shadow sighs behind me
like a ghost, like someone standing over me
while I scrub the tub. You never fully appear.
The door clicks in its latch, the heater kicks on,
the ice shifts in the freezer. The fork from your place
setting scrapes the plate but nothing is eaten.
I am haunted by a spirit who is too unobtrusive
when I'd rather your revenge, the scene where I pay
penance in terror for my crimes, but you aren't dead,
just gone. It feels the same. Even the dog has stopped
barking at the glimmer in the air when the sun shines
through. This is what they mean when they say a house
settles, when whatever is still there sinks in further,
no faster than a wall or a floor leans into the hole
that we call a foundation even when it's a grave.

Heirloom

Thomas Lawrance

I wasn't inheriting the old house, not quite yet. But Nana, wheeled reluctantly into a nursing home earlier that week, had declared it wasteful for the place to stand lonely and uninhabited. It was also closer to the museum than my own apartment. *You might as well move in*, Nana reasoned. *Keep the place warm.* I carried the last of the boxes into the hallway. Heavy with archaeology textbooks, half of them written by me.

An English developer had already been in touch, interested in flattening the property to make way for one of his luxury *inns*, as he insisted on calling his hotels. These evening views were just the thing to make up his mind. The property gave way in the west to a clearing in the trees. The Atlantic Ocean was a thin strand of blue thread on the horizon. The sunset illuminated the kitchen with a sleepy orange glow and turned that distant thread to lava. I pictured the old kitchen replaced by a shining five-star restaurant. Sleek worktops and luminous bars of stainless steel, steam fluffing from gigantic pots and expensive knives *chopping chopping chopping*. The fantasy blossomed around me—a waiter's arm balancing five dishes of tiny meals, a sweating chef accepting ferried compliments—but the kitchen instantly resumed its ordinariness when I saw Nana's battered old kettle. It was white, plastic, archaeologically stained with tea, three decades of the brand from which Nana never strayed. I was supposed to throw it away. And there was Jesus in his frame, warming a delicate hand over his immortal red bulb. I'd need to get rid of that, too. I'd do it soon.

A crucifix and a calla lily on the windowsill cast huge shadows on the wall. I'd spent more of the day at the nursing home than I'd intended, but Nana was a tireless storyteller.

"Did I ever tell you about the lovely old ash tree, Bridget? May 1972?"

"Did you ever tell me about the ash tree?" I said, smiling.
A member of staff handed me a paper cup of tea.

"The best stories bear repeating." Nana settled back in her
armchair, gazing out of the window. She inhaled deeply, ready
to reel off the tale, and then said simply, "They reversed over
the fucking thing!"

I laughed. I'd heard the story thirty times.

"A British army patrol," Nana continued, with emphat-
ic gestures, "tearing up the land with their big wheels and
stamping all over the crops with their boots. Wanted to check
if we were hoarding weapons. *No*, I told them, *but we've surplus
eggs if you want to take them back to your base.* And on their way
out, they backed right up to the ash tree and knocked it over.
Slammed down into the bog. Gone forever, the lovely ash tree.
A great-great-great-granddad planted that thing, you know."

"If it's any consolation, it's probably perfectly preserved,
however many feet down, unchanged from the day it fell." I
abandoned my cup of tea to the windowsill.

"Well, we'll never see it again."

"At least we can see the sunset from the kitchen now," I
said. "You can look out over the bog and watch the clouds red-
den on the mountains, and you can just make out the ocean.
Couldn't do that with a great big tree in the way."

Nana demurred. "No, but it's not safe down that way.
When you've settled in, keep away from the bog. Dangerous
spot. Watch the sunset from the kitchen," she added mater-
nally, "but don't wander down that way."

"I won't." By which I meant, *I won't settle in.* I decided to
fence off the bog before selling the place.

In the kitchen, I watched the sunset. From this vantage
point, safe in the silent house, the wide, lifeless bog looked sol-
id, a harmless oval of mud, but to step on its surface would be

---

fatal. An ancient quagmire of peat and water, it had once—as Nana was so keen on repeating—consumed an entire ash tree. This evening the sunlight glistened on it, and it divulged no hint of its contents. To look at it now, the tree might never have existed after all. My grandmother was an inventive storyteller.

The bog was exactly the sort of thing I'd enjoyed studying at college. Now I was an archaeologist with a post at the museum, and here was this beautiful bog sitting right there in the garden. The sun disappeared behind the violet mountains and the flaming sea. I switched on the outside light. The bog was dark and ethereal, as it appeared in my childhood nightmares. A mist seemed to be creeping in, but it might have been an illusion. I'd spoken to my colleagues about the bog. They agreed with me; it'd be an amazing site for investigation. A local peat bog dating back centuries, according to historical documents; perhaps even longer.

Heeding Nana's warnings, I'd never been down to the bog myself. In fact, out of a childhood respect, and a fear of its murky depths, I'd avoided the garden altogether. An owl landed in one of the surviving trees, watchful eyes gleaming, as if sent by Nana to keep an eye on me. I switched off the light.

The team assembled that weekend, early on Saturday morning. There were only three of us; myself and two colleagues I'd known since college. Colin finished his cigarette and flicked the butt into the muck of the bog.

"Colin, don't do that," I said. He shrugged apologetically and leaned over to retrieve the cigarette. "Colin, don't lean over the bog."

He stepped back altogether, rolling his eyes cloudward. "When's your man getting here?"

As he spoke, the ground rumbled, and a small digger appeared at the end of the drive.

"Colin, put the kettle on," I ordered. "Aoife, clear this area here. He needs to park up without falling in."

Colin and Aoife set about their tasks as I greeted the driver. I issued instructions, and soon the digger was scraping away at the surface of the bog, dumping great wet mounds of it on the garden.

"We might bump into a tree at some point," I said. "An ash. Quite recent."

The next morning, we did bump into something. "It's not a tree," Colin said helpfully.

A human body was set down on the grass. It had been scooped up by the digger in a great block of peat, Earth's offering of thick, dank coffin. Miraculously, only a hand and a foot were severed during the corpse's clumsy excavation; they remained in the bog, partially submerged. They could be retrieved later.

I wondered if this would affect the property's asking price.

"We need to store this body immediately," Aoife said. "Jesus. I was expecting farm tools and pottery. Colin, help me wrap this poor guy up. We'll transport him straight to the museum, tuck him straight into cold storage." The naked corpse was wrapped in plastic. Colin accompanied it in the back of the van as Aoife drove back to the museum. I dismissed the digger; we'd be busy enough for a while now.

Alone in the garden, I marveled at the situation. A bog body, here on Nana's old farm. A career-defining find. I'd have reports to write, interviews to give. TV appearances, even. But there was somebody I had to speak to first. There was an apology to be made.

"I told you not to go near it!"

"I know, and I'm sorry, Nana, I really am."

"You should have waited till I was dead."

The concerned expression of a nurse peered into the room. "Tea?"

"No, thank you. Nana, I know it was wrong, but look at what it's thrown up for me. The bog body exhibits have done so well up in Dublin. Now we'll have one here, in our little town! Think of that. What a legacy for your old farmhouse."

Nana was silent for a while, staring out of the window.

"How old are those bodies in Dublin?" she said eventually.

"That's the exciting thing," I enthused. "This guy could be five thousand years old! Carbon dating should give us a good estimate. Weirdly, we didn't find your ash tree, but I don't know—half these stories you tell me . . ."

"How accurate is this carbon dating thing?"

"Accurate enough," I said. "It'll tell us the century, at least."

Nana turned from the window to look at me and spoke quietly. "Then we're in trouble."

I felt my extremities go cold. "What?"

"July 20, 1972. Don't waste your time with this carbon dating thing. Thursday, July 20, 1972." We sat in silence. "It was self-defense, I should clarify," Nana added.

"Nana," I said slowly, "tell me this is one of your stories."

"Yes," Nana said. "One of the true ones. You weren't born, Bridget. You never met these people. You don't know what they were like. They wouldn't leave us be."

"What people?" Part of me hoped Nana was spinning some elaborate joke about Neolithic man.

"He was a British soldier. He came to the house. Your grandfather was at the market. Your mother was with him. The soldier got . . ." She looked around the room for the right words. ". . . very unpleasant. I struck him with a hammer. You'll find that, too, if you keep looking. Your grandfather came home. We sent your mother up to bed, she didn't see any of it.

Your granddad helped me strip the body and burn the clothes. It was my idea. We dropped the soldier in the bog, and he was swallowed up, like the tree two months before him."

I listened, openmouthed. "If it was self-defense . . ." I managed to stutter.

"You think these people gave fair trials? They suspected your granddad from the day they saw him. He used to shoot rabbits—they said he was a rebel for owning a rifle. No. It happened, it was a secret, and that was it. Officially missing. Still listed as such, I should imagine, if you care to do the research. Gone forever, I thought. Your granddad died thinking it would go to the grave with him. With us. Well. You've brought it to the bloody nursing home."

I sat back, exhaling for what seemed the first time in minutes. "I'll fix this," I said. "There are no identifying features. I'll fix this. I'll fix the dating."

"Good." Nana took a relaxed sip of tea, as though everything was immediately resolved.

"I'm going to go, Nana," I said, putting on my coat and stumbling toward the door. "I love you. I've got to hurry."

"Yes." Nana turned to the window, and then remembered something. "Oh, and Bridget? He was wearing a watch."

"What?"

"We burned his clothes, but your grandfather and I only noticed the glint on his wrist as he sank." I stared at her, and she continued. "Your ancient bog body is probably wearing a wristwatch."

The old lady resumed her window gaze.

Jesus. A Brit in the bog. I rushed to the museum and took the stairs three at a time to cold storage. There was nobody around. A wristwatch, for God's sake! Perhaps Aoife and Colin had found it, and had returned to the farmhouse already, bristling with suspicious questions. I yanked the drawer open and carefully unwrapped the corpse. Its face was pristinely preserved. There was a clear dent in the skull, under thick brown hair. I folded the plastic back, revealing the neck, the chest, the torso, the arms—

"Bridget?"

I wheeled around. "Oh, Colin, hi. Jesus, you gave me a fright."

"The ghost of the bog body." He waved his hands spookily. "What are you doing?"

"Just examining our friend here." I turned back to the corpse and unraveled the final concealing inches of plastic. One hand, one stump. No wristwatch. It must have been on the severed wrist. I relaxed instantly.

"I know, amazing, isn't it?" Colin stood beside me, looking down at the dead man. "He looks so . . ."

"Fresh."

"Exactly." Colin reached over and drew the plastic back up across the body. "And we need to keep him tucked in if we want him to stay that way." He closed the drawer. "We also need to pick up his missing parts, the hand and foot. We can do that tomorrow. They're not going anywhere."

Back at Nana's house, I switched on the outside light. Cramming all childhood instincts deep into my gut, I ventured to the very edge of the bog. In the gloom, two artifacts protruded from the murk. The first was only a meter or so away. Straining with a shovel, and careful to avoid leaning out over the bog, I managed to drag it up onto the grass. I sat down and, dabbing gently with reams of kitchen roll, removed sticky black globs of peat.

"Fucksake." In my hand was the man's severed foot. I threw it with some force back into the bog and picked up the shovel. The hand was further out than the foot had been. I leaned as far as was safe, and then further, but it was no use. I almost thought I could discern the wristwatch, glinting cruelly, goading.

I scurried up to the house and returned to the bog's edge with a length of hosepipe tied around my waist. I began muttering useless half-prayers, patchily remembered sentiments from school. I didn't want to leave another corpse in my grandmother's garden. Tightening the hosepipe, and gripping the shovel, I stepped cautiously into the peat.

The first few steps were deceivingly steady, but the moment my confidence lifted, my body began to descend. I sank down to my waist. I clung to the shovel as though it were a buoyancy aid, and I waded through the rising bog, reaching blindly ahead. I was up to my neck now; in a lightheaded moment I regarded this as apt. Finally, my fingers fell onto those of the dead man. With my other hand I abandoned the shovel and hauled myself back along the hosepipe, hoping that it wouldn't tear itself from the rusty fitting under the kitchen window.

I flopped down on the grass. The watch slid off the dead man's wrist into my palm. Nana's tale was confirmed. I wiped clean the unbroken face; it read ten past four. Ten past four on Thursday the twentieth of July 1972. Pocketing the watch, I threw the hand back into the bog and went inside. For decades the shower in the old farmhouse had only run cold, a judgmental sputtering half spray. Tonight, it was searing.

"Bridget!" Colin said, greeting me as I returned to work. I'd been away for a week and had missed much of the ceremony. "I was very sorry to hear about your grandmother."

"Thank you, Colin. It's fine. Lovely send-off yesterday. Wonderful lady."

"And how's the farmhouse? Handed over the keys to your man yet, with the hotels?"

"What? Oh, no," I said. I'd been ignoring the increasingly frantic emails and messages from the English developer, and eventually—in a final expletive-heavy voicemail—he'd abandoned his designs on Nana's farmhouse. "No, I've sort of settled in."

"Are you sure you don't need more time off?" Colin asked. "You've been so busy here the past couple of months, sorting out all the reports and the details. Almost single-handedly, too. Aoife and I should've been of more help."

"No, no," I assured him. "I love all that stuff. And I wanted to come and see your performance. I understand you've nominated yourself for tour-guide duties."

Colin laughed. "Nice watch," he said then, clocking the shining timepiece on my wrist.

"Thank you," I said. "Inherited."

"Grannies always leave the best heirlooms. Anyway, I'd better . . ." He jerked his head toward the exhibition room. "Third tour of the day."

"Go on," I said, and he hurried off to greet the latest group.

"How old is it?" a tiny voice asked. Twenty schoolchildren stared at the exhibit in thrilled disgust. The corpse, its midriff tastefully covered, lay on a plinth under gentle yellow lighting. The severed hand and foot sat by their respective stumps.

"Well," Colin said, "a special process called carbon dating—conducted by one of my colleagues here at the museum—tells us he died over five thousand years ago! And as you can see from this grisly diagram, his head bears signs of trauma. Perhaps the fellow was killed in a struggle," Colin suggested, with playfully grave intonation, "or some violent dispute over land."

alms

BEE LB

for Sue

i think of your body as it was, worn tough
and thickly muscled in the heat of the sun

clay clinging to your hands as you dig
for yourself a garden in the unrelenting

crust of weathered rock. i think of you
as you must have been; angry and determined

to find release. your body hunched over
earth, your fingers ungloved and digging

hard, the physicality of prayer with no
reverence to be found. not seeking to

find beauty, but to create it, and how
far from the mark you would fall.

i think of the strength found in your body,
how very much it would take to birth

what you did and continue on, unrepentant.
not without regret, but lacking the voice

to make it known. how grief replaced the son,
laying heavy and calm in your rounded belly.

how time withered your body
curling you down into nothing

as you raised your hand with both care and cruelty.
how your voice grew sharp, losing the warmth

of the arkansas sun. you made a home for
yourself in the swell of anger. your tendency

to coax life disappeared, swallowed by the life
given to you in bad faith; his mouth a careless hunger.

*not seeking to find beauty,
but to create it*

elusion

BEE LB

---

for my first uncle, Paul

i think of him as a lifeline,
whenever it is i think of him

what was it he said? *we bore ourselves deeper
'til we can't get out* the ache of regret bleeding
through even tone. a whole life lived
evading this wound

this line of sick trails through our shared history,
this vein of blood so thick it blocks movement

when asked if it's hereditary, she stops
says *yes* when she means *no*
easier to explain away than to admit

we each come to this constriction
on our own terms. no matter how bad
it gets, it can always get worse

there is nothing tender to be found
here, only raw and weeping
closed over with risk of reopening
healed poorly against a rigid scar

seeing in him the projection of my future,
familiar and aging, my fingers tremble
with the desire to trace frown lines,
smooth them over with something akin to hope

i wonder if his body feels as small and
cavernous as my own
if he cowers as i do, or if he's grown comfortable
in his cage of creation

does the sun offer him release, or some other form of capture
the right sight changes everything, and if i knew
he didn't hold this knowledge
i'd be the first to tell

we can't breathe but to breathe,
we can't breathe but for lack of breath

this heavy wonder, heavy shame
where does he hide his?
i'd love so dearly to compare

smooth them over with something akin to hope

breathe
grief

BEE LB

---

grief unbecoming, unending in its attempts
to pull air from lungs, replace it with salt.
a cure for those lacking the sweetness

of placebos. of course i'm still grieving.
i have reached out, again, again, and found
myself falling anywhere short of perfection.

sought by no one but myself, or so i've been led
to believe. the truth is grief has a way of curdling
anything it touches, and the longer it sits

inside you, the harder it is to keep it
from touching everything. my heart is heavy
with the burden of remaining. my mind spins itself

dizzy in efforts to forget. my memories weave
themselves together, a quilt of time material.
if i held the power to move on, i'd have

pulled myself from beneath the bath water,
dried my face and coughed up salt.
spat it out as my tongue cured, a new way

of speaking grief. but i'm still in the thick of it.
this body needing remedy to carry it out
of all the small deaths it's lived through.

this mind starting each day with the sun
through the water, every effort to
lighten the burden of being.

Introduction
to Napoleon

L Fulton

After the nightmare of familiar
weight and happy whispers crushing
my lungs, Napoleon's there
in his pajamas as I lie lost
and freezing in the snow.
He's not wearing a hat (his
hair twitches, is thin) and speaks

a language I don't understand.
I don't think he's real,
but nothing melts

at the realization. He sticks out
his hand, pulls me up. I am in
a world of blizzard and hills.
He hands me a hot cup,
guides me, French
still flowing. A few words
I recognize—Borodino,
chocolat, Josephine. The others
I do not know. I am in a house
of nothing but light and glass.
He says something, sounds
like a happy goodbye, it ends.

*

The book arrived after
the dream, 1,160 pages
of biography. I didn't order it.
I was expecting a set of whisks
and found his face staring out at
me from the box, a young man
who didn't know he'd be emperor,
his face smooth and untwisted by defeat.

Amazon couldn't tell me where
it'd come from, the rep apologetic
and confused, until he just hung up.

It was Thanksgiving so I was slicing
turkeys seventy hours a week, dreading
what I'd say to my family.
I read a chapter or two every night.

*

There is only one sketch
of Napoleon in St. Helena,
charcoal candid, his proud nose
turned down into a glum
bowl of porridge, the first emperor
of France confined to a lonely
rock in the Atlantic, a manor
musty with peeling blue wallpaper
four thousand miles from Paris.

He died at fifty-one, six years
after his exile, from tumors they'd find
only in the autopsy, the stomach
filled with what they listed as "coffee grounds,"
really the same sandy mix of blood
and bile they found in my grandpa's stomach.

This is how he visits me now, not fierce
and noble on an impossibly white horse
crossing the Alps, but that bold roughness,
scarfing down plain macaroni, stealing
chairs from his sitting room to make
the English officer that relayed him news
stand in his presence, drinking hot chocolate
with his secretary at 2 a.m. He sits
in my desk chair when I can't sleep,
telling me unintelligible stories about his
loves, his scholar's robes, the sea at Jaffa,
words harsh with comfort and violence.
It was better than being alone.

Living in an Abandoned House

Kika Man

Your ghost lingered in the door slightly ajar,
it did not matter anymore where you were

at this very moment—
all I could think about, the flowers we left in full bloom.

I still see the ghost of you. Upon touching
you, water from your clouds stuck to my skin.

Not my hands, but rosy burning
petals you threw in my direction.

If you are looking for a way out from this house,
then I am a window with a barren view.

I am cement-filled, gray matter overthinking. You,
the kitchen where we would bake pancakes on frozen mornings.

This world is melting as we go, but you found
a ship. Leave behind this house and your scent

in the creaks of my pillow—
my best friend I will never stop hugging in my sleep.

I will journal about you, the adventures
and teacups filled with romance in your future.

Perhaps to return one day, to the house
with the open doors and barred sights,

a hot beverage on the table,
chairs out. And then we can sleep.

白鬼

Kika Man

电梯开门
I have arrived at my very own room.
Wooden floor, soft mattress.
The difference is deafening, how do I
come home, how do I
leave this homesickness?

I left my head in China.
It got lost on the way here, like my luggage.
Unable to settle, we wander through films of earlier days.
Repetition, disconnection,
I couldn't find my keys, left dangling in elevator shafts.

Drag my head out of China, it got stuck
in the bars amidst the cigarette smoke.
Now I am surrounded by white ghosts,
I feed myself on memories of past times.
Unable to access this page with current connection.
电梯关门

Introversion

Kika Man

Day in day out, I
walk around my head
in the clouds; my feet
wandering purposeless; my eyes
resolute.

After the calm and the
planned, my heart and head
are still equally
beat up
with exhaustion.

The hundreds of feet
sharing the floors of
trains, restaurants, and escalators.
And the pairs of hands
holding their phones or
others' bodies attached
finger to finger.

Constant presence.
Relentless eye contacts,
immediately thrown away in embarrassment.
Or accompanied with a smile and a nod.

Cities that are alive
breathe through their citizens.
If you can't handle the shared
corpses walking around through their veins,
then why
did you come
?

Christmas Markets Close After New Year's

Emily Polson

—Budapest, Hungary

Our BlaBlaCar took a pit stop
in Győr, and the Polish-German driver
handed out shots of blueberry liquor
in the gas station parking lot
while he took his cigarette.

Yo hablé con el hombre de Argentina
and wished for his company over Julie's
as we navigated week two of traveling,
foreign tipping policies, and continental Europe's
oldest metro line.

Szabi, our guide, told us
of two national anthems:
   a hymn to God
   an appeal to the people
He prefers the latter for his country,
splintered in succession, battered
by Nazis and Soviets both.

In the world's second-largest synagogue
a man explained how a Christian architect,
a protestant pulpit, and an organ scandalized
Orthodox Jews but represented assimilation
for a people still clinging to the symbolic
presence of God in smaller numbers than before.

The memorial tree is a weeping, upturned menorah
and thousands are buried in twenty-four plots
but *Where heroes are not forgotten*
      there will always be more
So we went to the House of Terror
to be shocked and reminded.

But first, because we were tourists,
hedonists, humans, we passed an hour in
the most beautiful café in the world,
and when the pianist played
"All by Myself," I wondered why
I remember petty heartbreaks,
in light of all the pain in the world
            that is forgotten.

We spent the last of our forint
on two beers, goulash, and fried cheese
in a ruin pub papered with notes and ticket
stubs. We stuffed ourselves,
left something behind,
took a corner of the world
            with us.

January 2–5, 2017

*left something behind, took
a corner of the world with us.*

Lebkuchen Lattes at Alexanderplatz

Emily Polson

—*Berlin, Germany*

Our tour started at the hotel where Michael Jackson
dangled his baby out the window
and the presidential suite costs 15,000 euros a night
      no breakfast.

The goddess on the Brandenburg Gate
was first named for peace,
renamed for victory when
      Napoleon fell.

The Germans don't hide their history,
but memorialize genocide with a field of concrete
blocks in the city center (and around the markets
to stop anymore terrorists driving trucks through crowds
in the name of hysteria
      or something else).

No shrines for neo-Nazis, though—our guide
showed us the site of the Führer's
suicide bunker, a few meters below a
      poo-covered car park.

The parliament, too, sits below their people,
the Reichstag's ceiling a glass floor
they've already shattered, though I wonder
how many male MOPs look up skirts
of foreign women walking
      through the dome.

We smile at the East's happy Ampelmann
traffic light, a leftover of communist design
directing the proletariat; but we are beasts
of capitalism and habit, buying trinkets of him
            to take home.

        We are the people

eating currywurst
drinking blueberry glühwein
paying fifty cents to pee
crossing borders without thought.

Our country talks of building walls
not many years after they chanted

        We are one people

as they tore theirs down.

December 23, 2016

Our country talks of
building walls

they tore theirs down

A Heritage Erased

Marissa Alvarez

like most of my ancestors
their history is lost to me
it must have been backbreaking work
bending to their task
the sweat on their brow
the dirt on their hands
the calluses—the grit
the iron—the wood splinters
rock mountain tunnel ties rails
the strike of hammer to spike
mile after mile of track
carving and connecting the country
those hardworking traqueros
paid the least of all workers
didn't even have breathable fabrics
hopefully some cool water
perhaps pulled by a horse and cart
I can only imagine
it must have been difficult

almost as difficult
as when I look now and see
the story of railroad building across the U.S.
which in many ways is a microcosm of
the story of the U.S.
and I see my ancestors have
                    disappeared
from the narrative

almost as difficult
as wondering
(knowing)
from which narratives
I (we) will now
                    disappear

my ancestors have
                    disappeared
from the narrative

Tighten the Noose

Eddie House

Sun soaked, light raining down through the blinds we never closed. I don't know what it means to be haunting, only ever haunted. Kisses pressed to pressure points become cigarette scars on the inside of your wrists, a reminder of what it feels like to have love cremate into ash. Untangle limbs, untangle hearts, call you just another meaningless lover. Don't tell anyone that you bought hazelnut coffee to taste his lips again. Fall into bed on another sweat-bathed night and find redemption in the palms of his hands.

There's Healing and There's Creating

Eddie House

We're bathed in starlight across a dingy pub in a place we both call hometown. I'm sick with wanting or maybe that's the drink churning my stomach. Hesitant eye contact, neither of us makes the first move, and I'm clutching the fractures of ten years behind my back as if I didn't know you'd still be able to look through me like sea glass. Do you remember how I collected it for you on that beach in Spain? My hands stutter in a way they haven't for years and we're caught up in the flashing neon of a tacky dance floor and each jolt of changing light brings back another time and place we existed in. Remember when all the poems were about your eyes instead of my heart? I take a step forward, you spin like a missed dance step. Time passed us by a long time ago now but I'm back where I was, watching your back instead of holding your hand.

Ghosting

Amy Wang

On the last day in May of our senior year, you drive your red Mini Cooper into the railing overlooking the west bank of Lake Erie with the two of us in it. It is an accident, a brake confused for an accelerator, open air confused for the safety of a smooth road, not that it is any consolation to you, or Mom, or Dad, or any of the other people who weep over my open casket. (Or me, for that matter, as I stand in the corner of the funeral home next to the lilies and watch people say things about me that they would never have said when I was alive.) On Mom's kitchen countertops, on the cabinets Dad hand-made, on your shoulders, grief dimples like gray silk, but you brush it off and cough on the dust that flies up. After the second round of black-clad relatives leaves, you pack your powder-blue bags and buy a two-stop Greyhound ticket to the closest big city. When Dad asks where you're headed you tell him "college," and he nods and shuts himself back in the master bedroom. You read this as another sign of his disappointment, at you, the son he has never been able to find satisfaction in. It is only later you realize he'd spent the afternoon topping up your debit card, and by the time you do you are already two hours away in New York.

It has only been nineteen days since I stood up from the wreckage of that car crash but my body did not, only two weeks since they lowered my casket into wet earth, only a day since my girlfriend stood on our lawn and screamed herself hoarse at the shuttered front door. Yet as you lean into the musty cradle of the bus seat, I hover over you gently, my hands trellising through your short hair as home disappears over the horizon and smudges into asphalt. The last time I did this we were still two living children instead of one dead and one wishing to be, but for now I can only float, caught in reverie if nothing else.

By the time the bus reaches the station, it is mid-June and showering gently. Your umbrella is still at home in the broom closet and so you learn something new: the rain in New York is different from the rain back in Ohio, but on your tongue it tastes the same. Like salt. Like fingerpaint. Like your dead twin's face melting back into the steam of a bathroom mirror, leaving only your own staring back at you. On a wet park bench you wrap your arms around your knees and cry into your elbows, and I can only watch, my legs falling through wood as I try to shield you from the gazes of curious strangers. Their eyes cut right through me, and in a way, right through you, searchlights trailing themselves hollow in the chinks of your fingers.

In the bathroom of the apartment you rented off of Craigslist, you stare at yourself as the fluorescence of the exposed tile turns you pale. I can almost taste the longing suffusing your throat, I can almost choke on the desire that has locked inside my own. It has been a month since I last touched a living person, and my fingers ache with the loss of something I never knew I could miss. I stand behind you, feet stiff on unfamiliar grout, two hands outstretched as you trace a blade over your wrists. Your veins are hollow and ivy-green, threads thin enough to scatter with only a breath. I scream my soundless throat hoarse before you slip your hands back into your pocket and the razor back into your toiletry bag, but it is too little, too late, and I can see it for myself in the way your bones clatter gently with every finger that I pass through your spine. That night, you sleep on your side and I sleep on the kitchen counter, faux marble pressing my elbows into accordion folds. The next morning, as you lie wrapped in borrowed quilts, I realize that city sadness is hollow. It is empty hands and skylights that paint your face golden. It is dust motes sour with rain; half the sky wreathed with lemon-lime clouds and the other half flashing sullen, an evening alight in an orange halo between skyscrapers.

Underneath the glaze of a half-hidden sun, windowpanes melt into a glass slurry, and you stare at the soldiering lines of missed calls from Mom and cry. My number is still the first in your saved contacts; you have yet to unpin it. The smell of citrus and rain boots is always wet on your hands, fragrant and bittersweet and a reminder of heat-swollen summers from so long ago, when the two of us still existed on the same plane and I could still hold your hand in mine and you could still say *I have a twin brother* without flinching.

In New York, the two of us find that when cashiers give you your change back at the register it's in the degrees to radians that your body has shifted in the time between your first smile and your last one. You miss your soulmate by inches on city pavement, a centimeter too late and forty seconds too far to the left, and I watch her go, the two of us gusting past, one near-tethered and the other almost undone. I mourn for your missed chances and you mourn for me, every inch between the two of us a contradiction.

The days begin passing quickly; something stretches tight and taut the second my fingers glance off of yours, and I become another observer, the millionth cross-section of the white veil drifting over big cities. There are other ghosts here, men and women and little boys dragging stuffed animals down asphalt, hundreds of thousands of weightless bones turning mo(u)rning sky into milky mist, tethered to their living loved ones. The few times you muster up enough energy to get up out of bed, I trail after you as you track the same path down the city, waving hello to the ghosts of the girl whose mother died in a car crash, whose father unspooled himself into bone and unzipped carcass two days later on the freeway. The two of them spend evenings in the hallway of the apartment, people watching, and when I tell them what happened to the two of us, the mother clucks comfortingly and tells me I'll understand someday. Tells me I only have to wait until you stop needing me to pass beyond the veil. Tells me it gets better. Her voice is comforting, for what it's worth. Measured, like bone dice in pocket.

I smile at her, but deep down I cannot lean into her words with full confidence. I know all too well what it means to watch your twin spend a week's worth of cashiering on white wine from the corner deli and then two hours after that, be caught in a grief so heavy as to be immovable.

But it does get better. It takes eighteen months for you to forget the shape of my face, and it is only after you graduate that you remember it again. This time, I am not as airbrushed. Not as glazed with the halo of tragedy. You can look yourself in the mirror without seeing a boy who is already dead. For the first time in months you go outside onto the street, and the sunlight steeping on street corners feels like a benediction instead of a punishment.

You go to therapy. For the first time you finally seem to understand what it is that I have been trying to tell you since the moment my spine shattered like glass. That you can live without choking on atonement with every word. That it is not your fault. That my death is not the end of your life as well.

It is four years since we last spoke that you finally buy a plane ticket home. Your voice is low as you tell Mom you're coming back. On the other end she is choking, throat cut to fragments as she tries to speak. Distantly, you can hear the sound of your father sobbing, and this time he is crying for his youngest child, for the boy that he was on the verge of losing instead of the one that he did.

At the end of the call, in the back of your mind, you are thinking of me. Me, somewhere in the Midwest plains, wrapped in tall grass and a casket, the shattered window of my voice whispering gently in rows after rows of weeds. From the corner armchair I am standing on, I can already smell mothballs and choking salt. On my tongue, there is the bittersweet taste of letting go. As I close my eyes and you open them, I am grateful. Finally, that you're ready to move on.

Already, I can feel myself turning into dust. Release is gentle, I find. In my last moments, my eyes are filled with your smile. How lovely you look, breathing freely.

My Sisters
and I

Pim Wangtechawat

5. We drive and drive until we find a place where we can park and drink. We order nachos and onion rings and glasses of beer and vodka. I would prefer whiskey, but I have to drive. We are all a little jaded, a little short-changed, a little lost in the big city, in the whirlwind of early adulthood. Our twenties are more unkind than films and TV shows have promised them to be. We think we are grown-ups now.

(sort of, a little, maybe not at all.)

4. We talk about random things. Why men aren't like the men we imagine in our heads. Why we don't keep in touch anymore with the people we love. Why we need to get out of here—find new places to visit and appreciate. We mix the guacamole, the salsa, the cheese. We spin it all around and we laugh. We find nobody else funny anymore.

(and if we do, we don't say it.)

3. We talk about love and loss. We laugh about other girls because we are bitter and we've had a couple of drinks. Yes, the dull ache is still there, we say. The dull ache which means the want, the longing, the pain, the missing something we never had. Maybe we will be alone forever. Maybe we won't find anyone else. The future does not look too bright.

(if we think about it too much, we wouldn't be here.)

2. We take pictures in front of the bathroom against the brown bricked walls, and we walk outside with our arms wrapped around each other back to the car. At least we have us. Us— far away, close together, always orbiting around each other, always crying about one thing or another. We stroll through the aisles in the supermarket and share stories that we don't tell ourselves when we are happy.

(maybe we'll forget them if we tell them enough.)

1. We blast music as loud as we can in the car on the way home. Sing the songs at the top of our lungs. Who cares if they are sad songs—the ones we listen to when we want a good cry? Music tastes different when it is shared by more than one person. We don't say it out loud, but we know that we are all missing people who do not exist anymore.

Are we in love? Yes. Maybe a little. With ghosts and shadows and the notes that have disappeared into the warm, soft night.

(it is better to be broken together than not to be broken at all.)

with ghosts and shadows and the notes that have disappeared into the warm, soft night

Hua Hin

Pim Wangtechawat

My grandmother's touches were soft, tender and fragile.

Surprising
for a woman who had lived
through the lives of four kings
the second world war
the birth of four children
and the death of a husband.

I should have
asked her every question under the sun
instead of just
kissing her on the cheek
sitting down at her feet
and watching TV.

Because she is now nothing but empty spaces
in empty wicker chairs
in empty dusty rooms
in empty beach houses
and I am out
of memories.

It Goes
So Fast

Jen Gupta

I count eight dead raccoons on the way
and wonder if it's raccoon mating season
that drives them to the side of the highway.

Dad speaks to us morbidly. He says he'll be dead
by the time our two-year-old pup goes.
You'll only be seventy-five if she lives for ten more years,

Mom argues. *My father went at seventy-six,*
he says, *it all goes so fast.* Faster
if you're a raccoon, apparently.

You know, I still miss my father,
he says with pinot noir in his teeth.
In his eyes, I can see the reflection

of the people he is preparing to leave behind.
*It feels like yesterday he was pulling weeds
from our yard, Sarah still in your belly.*

Sarah sips nervously. I think of the drive down,
my full bladder and angry stomach,
the number of times I wished the clock faster.

It all goes so fast. This moment here, this unfamiliar
glimpse at grief, this wine-soaked conversation.
In the morning, the memory is fuzzy and when I hug him

goodbye, I let go slower. On the drive, I count
each dead raccoon, but I do not count the minutes
and it goes so fast.

The
Black
Dog

Bianca Grace

The black dog sat in our home
at your bedroom door and attacked
the chemicals in your brain

each time you attempted to make an escape
to freedom. The black dog was your accomplice
when you were sentenced

to two months in a psych ward
for choking back a sleeve of Valium.
In a high security

ward hallway, you wept
to me through your old
Nokia flip phone *I'm dead set certain*

I'm dying
anyway. You depicted
how the nurses rummaged

through your personal belongings
and cackled harder than the riddles
of thoughts that plagued your cerebrum

for twelve weeks. They peeked
into your room like children
playing hide and seek

but it was no game
to you. You whispered
of the bittersweet moment

the social worker spoke my name
and the memory
surfaced of the days you drove

me to school and held the traffic
up like road works with permanent stop
signs. It was the only way

you could make me laugh
on Monday mornings driving
through the highway to hell.

When you were transferred to a nursing
home, your name was slammed
with block letters across the head

of your door
and the color of the panel
reminded me of the peanut

butter you ate by the spoonful.
After I walked into your room,
I watched the wrinkles

become deeper than any mistake
you had made in the past
eighty years. But I saw your temper

that painted the walls
red and yellow never lost the spark
when I transformed into a ghost

with my mask.
I untied my disguise
so you could see I wasn't hiding

from you, I just needed time to heal
myself and realize it wasn't me
you were trying to leave.

Fortunate Father

Elle Hammond

I see so much of my father when I look at myself.
Being in a perpetual state of grief for him—though he is still living—makes this hurdling. Someone at one of the tennis clubs he worked at when I was a teenager mentioned I was simply "Jim, but with curves," which I'd find to be, awkward of a statement as it was, true. We both have dimpled chins and long fingers and toes, round eyes and thick hair. We're tall, mostly legs. When I do calf raises or squat jumps, I think of him if I catch myself in the mirror; my knees somehow look exactly like his.

I don't play tennis much anymore (I once joked that this made me feel like Prince Harry, as if my quietly leaving the sport after going no-contact with my father were anything like a royal departure), but when I get the chance, I think of my dad. Tennis wasn't all we did together, but it sure was the glue. Him being a pro, I could rarely earn a point against him.

Sometimes, though, I'd place a shot on the edge of the line, right in the corner to where it was 99 percent out but 100 percent in, and *sometimes*, he'd miss it. When that happened, he got this phony Three Stooges angry grin and would start running toward me, rolling up his sleeves as if now it were *really* on. It started as a joke when I was small, but the humor never overripened (and he always loved an audience). When he got to the midpoint of the court, he'd casually step over the net as if he didn't even see it there and keep heading my way.

My father was the tallest person I've ever known.

He's not old now, but he looks it—he has only some of his most noticeable physical traits remaining, and they're covered up by new installments that make it hard to see that, yes, this person used to be handsome. There are more common signs of aging, like his gradually hunching back and his not-so-gradually graying hair, then there are the ones that could happen to only him. He's missing a lot of teeth now. I don't know why; don't really want to ask.

Whenever it comes up that my father is in a nursing home, I almost always want to defend it with, "but he wasn't *always* there," which, if you were to think about it for even a fraction of a second, goes without saying. But I do feel I have to qualify it. People seem to think that maybe he's older than his midsixties, that he's there for an unfortunate but perfectly natural reason. If someone is curious enough to ask, they generally do not like the answer that he's there because his decades of alcohol addiction ate some of his brain, which is the layman's summary for Wernicke's encephalopathy.

Chronic conditions—like addiction—are funny, because there was never a "moment" when I realized my father was an alcoholic. I always knew never to touch Dad's drink on the tennis court, even if I was *really* thirsty. I knew, when I got older, that sometimes I'd have to pick him up or drive us home from a restaurant he'd taken us to. I knew he was a local celebrity at nearly every bar he took me to, that his drinks transformed him into the perfect crowd-pleasing balance of Greek hero and clown. None of this was odd. Some of it was thrilling, even ethereal; I'm sure everyone would want to be looked at the way the barflies looked at my dad.

I wonder who all looks at him now. Now, his room at the home is small and cold. I'm always chilly, so when I prepared to visit him and to see him for the first time in years, I brought an extra jacket, but the room is still cold. The air conditioning is on despite it being late autumn. It doesn't seem to bother him. He and I have just hobbled and walked (respectively) through a hallway decorated like an elementary school, with construction paper chains strung around doorways and crafted snowflakes and snowmen to celebrate the coming holidays.

For the most part, the room is empty. There's a hospital bed pushed all the way up against a small television stand so he can be as close to it as possible; he sits on the bed with his legs stretched out and leans forward to watch it, and I see the telltale psych ward socks stick out from under a thin sheet. Across the room waits a nightstand in the corner with nothing on it. In his closet hang some clothes and shoes I recognize from when we lived together in an apartment, and I wonder how he got them. The last I'd heard, he didn't have much after getting evicted years prior. No lights are on, save for the blue glow from the television. My request to change that is quickly vetoed.

Dad will occasionally turn to look at me during our visit, sometimes to ask me questions but mostly to tell me facts about the hockey game we're watching—he knows all the players' names, if they used to play for another team, and some of their good (or bad) moments on the ice. We're flipping back and forth between a St. Louis Blues game and a rerun of *NCIS*, the criterion for switching being whichever one isn't airing commercials at the moment. Because of this, we miss moments from each—points scored, clues gained. I notice, but I don't think he does. He's glued nonetheless.

"What do you like to do here?" I ask, assuming they have activities like bingo or bridge.

He shrugs. "Well, I don't sleep much. Too much to do. They play *Friends* and *Seinfeld* reruns at night on one of the channels, and luckily shows like *NCIS* run a lot during the day. Then there's always ESPN to watch." He turns up the volume but complains that the remote hasn't adjusted anything.

I'm still eyeing that nightstand. "Maybe I could get you some flowers," I suggest. It's feeble. I backtrack. "Or a picture or two?"

"What?" he replies. He doesn't look up.

"Pictures, you know? Like, of us. Or of you. Or Grandma."

"*What?*" he asks again, and I start to realize that maybe it wasn't him mishearing. We go back to *NCIS*. He's still fiddling with the remote, telling me it's broken (it's not—I see the buttons he presses take effect on the screen—but according to him, it is). I need to get him a new remote, he insists. I promise him I will look into it.

I ask who comes to visit him, and he shrugs. "Nobody, I guess." I shrug, too. I think I get it.

We're already out of things to talk about, and I'm terrified to ask him about himself. I don't fully understand why he's here, or how he arrived.

When I last saw him nearly five years prior, I told him to never speak to me again. I had just graduated college after spending the better part of it traveling between school and home to balance Dad's affairs. His addiction had gotten bad: there was time spent in rehab, time spent incarcerated, evictions, getting thrown out of bars, getting fired, juggling relationships with multiple women at one time. I came home one weekend to find my childhood cat dead since Dad went to jail unexpectedly and I was stuck at school. When people tell me I'm too young to have a knee that snaps and pops this much, it takes everything for me not to fire back, "Well, I fucked it up trying to drag a 250-pound man away from the toilet since he'd fallen asleep with his head in it." Petty as it is, I resent the "magna" preceding "cum laude" on my college diploma, knowing it would likely have been "summa" had I been able to make it to more classes instead of rushing home to peel my father off the floor.

No one else would help him. His mother had died; most other family lived out of town. Other family and friends gave

me the same "He's just going through a phase" runaround,
ignoring or enabling. Others just disappeared when they accepted that it wasn't a party anymore. It was infuriating, until
three years passed and I realized that perhaps everyone else
already knew what it took me that long to face: my dad never
asked to get pushed uphill every day, and he wasn't interested
in reaching the top. He was popular, handsome, and athletic,
and he may have been the tallest man most of us ever knew,
but he was an addict. He had been since before I was born.

After I graduated, I was tired. I told him to leave me alone.
And I'm not sure why, but he listened—I didn't hear from him
for years, save for a voicemail once on my birthday. My aunt
called a few summers later to let me know he'd gone to live
in a nursing home after a "binge he didn't bounce back from"
and where the home was. I didn't know much more than that
at first.

Now, he sits in a hospital bed pushed up against a TV
set, his legs splayed out like a child, complaining about the
remote; his feet twitch and he has no front teeth and he gets
excited about the small bag of Cheetos the staff gives him
each night at 8 p.m. along with his grab bag of meds.

I can already anticipate my friends' and other family's
response to this after I leave: a gentle "Well, what did you
expect?"

Good question. The romantic in me wanted to think
of his addiction as something like a cancer battle: I'd rally
around him while he went through hardships and hit his rock
bottoms only to come out on top. He'd beat alcohol and we'd
move on, my "real" dad coming back after a painful but tem-
porary interruption.

Truthfully, however, I expected him to die. I did not *want*
that. But Dad showed me in so many ways over so many years

that it was easier for him to remain addicted than to confront it, and I could only envision one way out. I was fully prepared for that phone call.

But *this* isn't right. This is somehow both and neither, and I can't piece it together. His commitment to watching his shows lets me stare at him all I want, like I'm refreshing the page and hoping for something to load properly. This is not anyone I've ever seen before, in body or mind, and yet it is my father's body, living, persisting.

I want to shake his saggy, hunched-over frame until he irons out and stands up tall and cracks a joke with me. Why is it *that* part that died, and what exactly did it leave? I require a linear timeline and log of where all the pieces I knew of him went and when they left him. At what specific point in addiction does the brain trade wit for obsession over a television remote? When does an audience eager for a story become less interesting than the Boomer version of *Paw Patrol*? And when I see my legs in the mirror or my shoes' skid marks on a clay court after a match, who else am I supposed to see?

After the hockey game ends, I decide to call it a night. He says I can come watch television with him anytime, and I thank him. As he walks me to the home's front door, I ask if I'm ever allowed to take him out for a visit; he hesitates but says he thinks I am, so I suggest we go out for a pizza next time.

He says *no*.

"You . . . *don't* want to go get pizza with me?" I balk.

"Mmmm, I don't know. Well, no. I don't think so. You could bring us one, but I really have to do a lot around here."

"What, your shows?" I can't hide my incredulity. "You don't want to get out of this place for a couple of hours?"

He finally makes eye contact with me; it's his turn to balk. "Why would I?"

He holds our gaze as I struggle to think of what to say first, but then I look more closely at him than I've been able to tonight. His eyes—they aren't bloodshot or glassy. They're clear; they look like mine now. I can't remember the last time I'd seen his eyes clear. I think about it: he's been in this home for almost two years at this point, making it the longest he's gone without a drink. And in his small room where I am cold and can barely see, he has what he needs; it's fortunate for him that he's here instead of in the wild (or worse). This is the only space in the past forty years where he's been consistently sober. Everything outside of it means addiction, so, yes, why would he want to leave?

This is the first time in my own life I've ever seen him sober. I concede in an instant that everything I've known of him before tonight—good or bad—was soaked in vodka. This person, unusual as he might be, isn't.

I accept the offer to bring him a pizza, and we hug good-bye. I suspect he'll appear strange to me from here on out. He is certainly different, but he is neither less than nor more than the person I knew before; he has not disappeared. He is new. And it's nice to meet him.

Rx: 2501

Judas Ātman

on the northbound train
i rake my memories against my arms
hoping the gentle rock
may lull me to sleep
—but in my dreams
i still see your disfigured face

it's not easy
to paint an image of a ghost
and the longer you left
the less real you became
in your wake
a bitter seed fell to the roots
rotting our garden
that lies in the depth of me since forgotten

i asked the pharmacy
if they had any forgiveness
and under a forgotten bridge
i tried to thread it through my veins
but the needle doesn't penetrate
to the heart of you
so i sit here unraveling
and wonder
if any stray thread remaining
will connect back to me
or if i am forever lost
to those years that fell before
engorging themselves on the outline of my shadow

swallowing what was left of my body
my name itself no more
than a piece of blame
to hurl across the dining table

it seems useless
to bring up an unchanging past
but the ache in my shoulder
is becoming unbearable
and the only way out seems to be
in the abyss between my dream
and waking up to you
looping
like a garbled word
having lost its meaning
when repeated once too many times

i used to hate you
but somewhere along the way
i stopped

i think i just got tired.

*it's not easy to paint
an image of a ghost*

Ghosts of Autumns Past

Vera Ene Oko

My parents are divorced but
they are still married when you scan my queer body
my eyes are father's sitting stern
in my oval face
and
my lips are mother's
pouty
            soft
                        seeking something . . .
other than mothering
father was once woman and mother once a man
and neither could forgive each other
for hiding the truth until now
my arms are slender and smooth
like mother's too
and my hands are father's
rough like tree bark
we still have family brunches in autumn
the sun plasters itself on the ground
in beds of golden fallen leaves
            on the dinner table
two more ghosts than before.

The Echo House

Eleri Denham

There's an oak-lined street where the tarred cracks in the asphalt resemble a map of rivers and tributaries, or a network of veins, depending on how you look at it. At the end of the street is the Echo House. It's a gingerbread Victorian, the kind that was out of date before it was built. A hundred midwestern winters have muted its colors, made it into a faded photograph of itself.

Cora lives in the Echo House. She has lived there a long time—not all of its hundred winters, but more of them than not.

In the dust-rimed living room Cora sits in a bony armchair and looks pensively into the cold fireplace. There the clatter of generations' worth of afternoon gatherings floats like ash, hanging in the shafts of hollow sunlight. The sounds—clinking porcelain, coffee being poured, the burble of relaxed conversation—have taken the shape of these tiny, weightless nothings. If she let enough of them collect on her fingertips, they would feel like silk.

Meanwhile in every corner laughter shimmers iridescent and trembling like cobwebs beaded with dew. The legacy of sorrow is heavier: it condenses along the walls, slides downward and forms puddles and warps the floorboards. Wherever paint curls up from the ceiling is the barking of dogs. Some of the dogs were Cora's. Some weren't. But she was taught to tell their barks apart, even the ones that were before her time.

On the kitchen counter she has an old cookie tin full of Christmas mornings—wrapping paper being torn, unfurling choruses of laughter and thank-yous—every one as delicate as a beetle's wing. Around each post of the banister is coiled the crying of a different baby, all of them long since grown. Dozens of exuberantly off-key renditions of "Happy Birthday" nest behind the china cabinet like stubborn, dissonant mice.

The windows, after so many years of springtime storms, have taken on a silver-blue film, the residuum of thunder.

Often, in the past, people danced in this living room. Cora sometimes hears the cadenced memories of their movement, captured in the subtly shifting patterns on the threadbare Persian rug. Their footfalls, though disembodied, make her smile. Some of those people are gone, and some of them simply don't dance anymore, but the Echo House still remembers. And for that Cora is grateful.

*the sounds have
taken the shape*

*of these tiny,
weightless nothings*

embers, dying

clementine valerie black

the porch swing only rusted when you let it. now, you sit on the damask cushions, push off, and brace yourself for the squeak. you wait for the wolf spider to pop out of the den under the rosebush. you wait for the double knot in your stomach to untease. it is dusk at your grandmother's house and her voice is missing, telling you to put on a sweater, telling you to leave the door open, but close the screen. the grass has gone yellow-brown and sweet. you are thinking about the endings. about ashes, headstones and flags, how long it has been since you stopped visiting. about thanksgiving, electric knife whirring, something brushing against you under the tablecloth, the smell of candied yams and slow-cooked meat. how do you break your mother's heart? how do you leave the hurt buried under the tree? the tree that never grew as tall as it was supposed to, that was always struggling. you study the holes in its brittle, russet leaves, and realize that it is sick. it is dying. there is no one to fuss over the state of the yard, the house is empty. the night is rolling in, there's a new sharpness on the edge of the breeze. you know you should go inside, but you can't bring yourself to turn the key. you sit, you shiver, you swing. you get up, start the car. drive to the walmart and you're navigating numb through the aisles, your hand closes around the smooth metal of a can of WD-40, and it is at that very moment that the dam breaks. it is at that very moment that you know you are free. you are a heap of black silk, shuddering with laughter and tears splashing cold tile. shoppers steer full carts around you, quietly. it is over. you wipe the mascara tracks from your cheek, straighten your skirt. you get up, place the can back on the shelf. brush yourself off. this is how you leave.

Contributors

Marissa Alvarez lives in a desert, misses snow and beaches, due to health moved back in with her parents, and enjoys their company and that of their shih tzu and the three cats they rescued together.

Denise Nichole Andrews, MFA, is the publisher of *The Hellebore Press* and founder of HUES. She teaches and resides in Sacramento, California, with her partner of ten years. Her writing and photography can be found in *Hooligan Mag* and *Parentheses Journal*. She enjoys lavender lattes, thrifting for interior and fashion finds, and being a friend to all. For tender tweets and affirmations, follow Denise on Twitter at @DNicholeAndrews.

Judas Atman (he/they) is a queer, mixed-race, South/Southeast Asian diasporic artist born and raised in San Francisco and now based in New York City. Their artistic practice is based in hybridity, including but not limited to performance, directing, and creative writing. In his work, he uses the liminality of his identity as a foundation for exploring the possibilities of becoming. In 2019 Judas graduated from NYU Tisch School of the Arts with a BFA in drama and a minor in film production. Since graduating, Judas performed in *LIFE* with Silver Glass Productions and was featured as a fellow in Theater Mitu's Hybrid Arts Lab.

clementine valerie black is a poet, teacher, and survivor. She has been published in *Honeyfire Literary Magazine*. She grew up in the shadows of Dallas, Texas. She lives with her husband, their dog, and a little black cat.

Maggie Bowyer (they/them/theirs) is a poet, cat parent, and the author of *The Whole Story* (2020) and *When I Bleed: Poems about Endometriosis* (2021). They are a blogger and essayist with a focus on endometriosis and chronic pain. They have been featured in *Bourgeon*, *Germ Magazine*, *Detour Ahead*, *Written Tales*, *Scribe*, and more. They were the editor-in-chief of *The Lariat Newspaper*, a quarter finalist in Brave New Voices 2016, and a Marilyn Miller Poet Laureate.

Nora Boyle is a poet, farmer, beekeeper, and witch who consumes coffee by the cauldron-full. She is the founder of Lady Book Witch Press, based out of New Hampshire, which produces limited edition artist books, letterpress broadsides, *Tiny Spells Witchery* collaborative how-to books, and the literary magazine *The Cackling Kettle*. Her website is ladybook witchpress.com. You can find her work on Instagram at @ladybookwitch.

Bethany F. Brengan (she/her) is a freelance writer and editor who splits her time between the Olympic Peninsula and the internet. Her poetry has appeared in *Channel*, *Solum Journal*, *Gordon Square Review*, *2015 Poet's Market*, and *CV2: The Canadian Journal of Poetry and Critical Writing*. She can be found at medium.com/essays-no-one-asked-for.

Rachel Bruce is a poet from Hitchin, United Kingdom. Her work has appeared in *The Telegraph*, *Second Chance Lit*, *Eye Flash Poetry*, *Eponym Magazine*, *The Daily Drunk*, and *The Hysteria Collective*. Find her on Twitter at @still_emo.

Michael Colbert loves horror films (his favorites are *Candyman* and *The Silence of the Lambs*) and coffee (his favorites are

Ethiopian and Costa Rican). He's an MFA student in fiction at UNC Wilmington, and his writing appears in *Electric Literature*, *Gulf Coast*, and *Atlas Obscura*.

Eleri Denham (she/they) writes fiction, nonfiction, and screenplays. Her work has appeared or is forthcoming in *Little Patuxent Review*, *Whale Road Review*, *Cease*, *Cows*, and elsewhere. Originally from Chicago, Eleri now lives in Oregon with her partner. Find her on Twitter at @eleri_denham.

Betty Doyle (she/her) is a poet and student from Liverpool, United Kingdom. She is studying for a PhD in creative writing at Manchester Metropolitan University, researching infertility poetry and writing her own. Her debut poetry pamphlet, *Girl Parts*, will be published with Verve Poetry Press in March 2022. For more of her work, find her on Twitter at @betty_poet.

L Fulton is a writer from Northeast Ohio. They just earned their MFA from BGSU.

Bianca Grace (she/her) is a student and poet from Australia. Her work has appeared in *Anti-Heroin Chic*, *Selcouth Station*, and *Ample Remains*.

Carol Coven Grannick is a children's author and poet with a 2020 debut novel in verse, *Reeni's Turn*, and multiple poems and short fiction in *Cricket*, *Highlights*, *Ladybug*, *Babybug*, *Hello*, and *Hunger Mountain*. Her most recent work for adults appears in a number of literary magazines, including *West Texas Literary Review*, Oprelle Publications's *Matter* anthology, *Red Coyote*, *2018 Mizmor Anthology*, *Otherwise Engaged*, *A Moment of Your Time*, and more. Her upcoming chapbook, *Call Me Bob*, is contracted with Oprelle Publications. As a columnist and re-porter for online journals and blogs, she chronicles the inner life of the writer and the creative process.

Jen Gupta is a middle school English teacher, writer, avid hiker, and horse lover. She lives in Somerville, Massachusetts, with her husband and their houseplants. Her work has been published in *Anti-Heroin Chic* and is forthcoming in *Sledge-hammer Lit.*

Elle Hammond lives in St. Louis, Missouri. She holds de-grees from Drury University in writing and English.

Eddie House is a twenty-four-year-old genderqueer manic pixie daydream. They enjoy writing, roller-skating, and get-ting very very drunk. Most likely to be found smoking out of a bedroom window or lying on the sofa complaining. You can find more of their work at *ImageOutWrite*, *Anatolios Magazine*, *Hustling Verse*, or tucked inside library books.

Kara Knickerbocker is the author of the chapbooks *The Shed-ding Before the Swell* (dancing girl press, 2018) and *Next to Every-thing That Is Breakable* (Finishing Line Press, 2017). Her poetry and essays have appeared in or are forthcoming from *Poet Lore*, *Hobart*, *Levee Magazine*, and *Portland Review* and the anthologies *Pennsylvania's Best Emerging Poets*, *Crack the Spine*, and more. She lives in Pennsylvania where she writes with the Madwomen in the Attic at Carlow University and co-curates the MadFridays Reading Series. Find her online at karaknickerbocker.com.

Thomas Lawrance is from the United Kingdom, but he lives in Ireland, where he writes fiction and performs stand-up comedy. His writing has appeared with *Bandit Fiction*, Brain Mill Press, *Montana Mouthful*, *The Bookends Review*, and others.

BEE LB is an array of letters, bound to impulse; they are a writer creating delicate connections. They have called any number of places home; currently, a single yellow wall in Michigan. They have been published in *Crooked Arrow Press*, *Badlung Press*, *opia*, and *Revolute*, among others. Their portfolio can be found at twinbrights.carrd.co.

Xiaoly Li is a poet, photographer, and computer engineer who lives in Massachusetts. Prior to writing poetry, she published stories in a selection of Chinese newspapers. Her photography, which has been shown and sold in galleries in Boston, often accompanies her poems. Her poetry is forthcoming or has appeared in *Spoon River Poetry Review*, *The American Journal of Poetry*, *PANK*, *Atlanta Review*, *Chautauqua*, *RHINO Poetry*, *Cold Mountain Review*, *J Journal*, and elsewhere. She has been nominated for Best of the Net twice, Best New Poets, and the Pushcart Prize. Xiaoly received her PhD in electrical engineering from Worcester Polytechnic Institute and her master's in computer science and engineering from Tsinghua University in China.

Kika Man 文詠玲 is a writer and a student from Belgium, and also from Hong Kong. She has always been writing and playing and learning and reading. To them, all of these are one and the same. Kika writes about mental health, traveling, and dreaming, about her mixed identity, about music and blueness. Alongside writing poetry, she is part of Slam-T, a spoken word and slam poetry platform. They have majored in Eastern languages and cultures: China at Ghent University and are currently chasing after a degree and PhD in gender and diversity and cultural studies.

Cassie McDaniel has published poems and fiction in *Human Parts*, *Used Furniture Review*, *Split Quarterly*, and *The Mangrove Review*. She lives north of Orlando. Say hi on Twitter at @cassiemc.

Sheleen McElhinney is a poet/baker living in Pennsylvania with her family. Her debut book, *Every Little Vanishing*, will be released in October 2021 with Write Bloody Publishing.

Sheila Mulrooney has an MA in English literature from the University of Toronto. Her work has appeared or is forthcoming in magazines such as *Typishly*, *Not Very Quiet*, *Dappled Things*, *The Agonist*, *The Society of Classical Poets*, and *America Magazine*.

Vera Ene Oko is a recent master's graduate of the University of Jos. When she is writing and even when she is not writing, she is mothering the smartest two-year-old, Kimberly, her muse.

Emily Polson holds a BFA in creative writing from Belhaven University and has been published in *Catfish Creek*, *Book Riot*, and *the Brogue*. Originally from Central Iowa, she now lives in Brooklyn and works in book publishing. You can follow her on Twitter at @emilycpolson.

Corinna Schulenburg (she/her) is an artist and activist committed to ensemble practice and social justice. She's a white queer transgender woman, a mother, a playwright, a poet, a founding creative partner of Flux Theatre Ensemble, and the director of communications at Theatre Communications Group. As a playwright, actor, director, and community builder, Corinna has worked on over forty plays in New York City and across the country. Find her online at corinna schulenburg.com.

JR Starzynski is a poet living in Columbus, Ohio. They have presented poetry at the Columbus Arts Festival and ComFest, and they were a featured reader for The Poetry Forum's reading series.

Emily Uduwana (she/her) is a California-based poet and artist. Her work has appeared in recent issues of *The Northridge Review*, *Stonecoast Review*, and *Pensive: A Global Journal of Spirituality and the Arts*. She can be found on Twitter at @em_udu.

Kalisse L. Van Dellen writes about where she's been and what she's lost. She is a graduate of Belhaven University in Jackson, Mississippi, and currently resides as a Canadian expatriate in Greenville, South Carolina. Her work has been featured in *the Brogue*, *The Du Bois Review*, and *Mississippi's Best Emerging Poets*.

Amy Wang is a writer from California. In her free time, you can find her reading fanfiction. Her work is published or forthcoming at *Twin Pies Literary*, *Ogma*, and *X-R-A-Y Literary Magazine*.

Pim Wangtechawat (she/her) is a writer from Bangkok with a master's in creative writing from Edinburgh Napier University. Her writing has been published in various places, including *Mekong Review*, *Nikkei Asian Review*, and *The Selkie*. She has performed her poetry at events in Edinburgh hosted by *Shoreline of Infinity* and the Scottish BAME Writers Network and has given talks about her writing at Chulalongkorn University and Ruamrudee International School. She is working on her debut novel *The Moon Represents My Heart* and is represented by Liza DeBlock of Mushens Entertainment. Follow her on Twitter at @PimsupaW and on Instagram at @pim.wangtechawat.

Editorial
Staff

Natasha Lioe, Founder and Publisher

Natasha Lioe graduated with a BA in narrative studies from University of Southern California. She's always had an affinity for words and stories and emotions. Her work has appeared in *Adsum Literary Magazine*, and she won the Edward B. Moses Creative Writing Competition in 2016. Her greatest strength is finding and focusing the pathos in an otherwise cold world, and she hopes to help humans tell their unique, compelling stories.

Carolina VonKampen, Publisher and Editor in Chief

Carolina VonKampen graduated with a BA in English and history from Concordia University, Nebraska, and completed the University of Chicago's editing certificate program. She is available for hire as a freelance copyeditor and book designer. For more information on her freelance work, visit carolina vonkampen.com. Her writing has appeared in *So to Speak*'s blog, *FIVE:2:ONE*'s #thesideshow, *Moonchild Magazine*, and *Déraciné Magazine*. Her short story "Logan Paul Is Dead" was nominated by *Dream Pop Journal* for the 2018 Best of the Net. She tweets about editing at @carolinamarie_v and talks about books she's reading on Instagram at @carolinamariereads.

April Bayer, Reader

April Bayer is an MA student in English literature at the University of South Dakota. She graduated with high distinction from Concordia University, Nebraska, in 2019 with a BA in English and theology and a BS Ed in educational studies. When she isn't busy teaching her students about literature and composition, she enjoys writing poetry, playing with cats, and researching the works of Willa Cather. Her work has previously appeared in *Potpourri* and *Capsule Stories Isolation Edition*. April joined *Capsule Stories* as a reader in November 2020.

Stephanie Coley, Reader

Stephanie Coley is a country girl from Gering, Nebraska. She graduated in 2016 from Concordia University, Nebraska, with a BA in English and a minor in art. She has been a journalism teacher, janitor, data technician, and more. Stephanie is a published poet, appearing in the National Creativity Series of 2009 and *Mango* Issue 3, Respeto, in 2017. She is also a winner of the 2020 Historic Posters Reimagined Project, which can be found at the Nebraska History Museum in Lincoln, Nebraska. Stephanie currently works as the program manager at the West Nebraska Arts Center in Scottsbluff, Nebraska. Stephanie joined *Capsule Stories* as a reader in January 2021.

Rhea Dhanbhoora, Reader

Rhea Dhanbhoora worked for close to a decade as an editor and writer before quitting her job and moving to New York to get her master's degree and finally writing the stories everyone told her no one would ever read. Her work has appeared or is forthcoming in publications such as *Sparkle & Blink, Awakened Voices, Five on the Fifth, Capsule Stories Autumn 2020 Edition, Fly on the Wall Press, HerStry, Artsy, Broccoli Mag,* and *JMWW*. Her work has been nominated for a Pushcart Prize and Best American Essays. She is currently on the board of directors for the literary organization Quiet Lightning and editor of RealBrownTalk. Rhea joined *Capsule Stories* as a reader in January 2021. She's working on several projects, including a linked story collection about women based in the underrepresented Parsi Zoroastrian diaspora. You can read her work online at rheadhanbhoora.com.

Hannah Fortna, Reader

Hannah Fortna graduated in 2016 from Concordia University, Nebraska, combining her passion for the written word and her affinity for art making with a degree in English and a minor in photography. After a three-year career as a freelance copyeditor, she heard traveling calling her name and now works seasonal jobs in places connected to America's national parks. When she's not selling souvenirs to tourists in gift shops, she enjoys hiking, photographing natural spaces, and writing about the flora and fauna she saw while on the trail. She reads anything from poetry to middle-grade novels, but the nature-inspired creative nonfiction section is her haunt in any bookstore. Her poetry has previously appeared in *Moonchild Magazine* and *Capsule Stories Spring 2019 Edition*. Hannah joined *Capsule Stories* as a reader in November 2020.

Kendra Nuttall, Reader

Kendra Nuttall is a copywriter by day and poet by night. She has a BA in English with an emphasis in creative writing from Utah Valley University. Her work has previously appeared in *Spectrum*, *Capsule Stories*, *Chiron Review*, and *What Rough Beast*, as well as various other journals and anthologies. She is the author of the poetry collection *A Statistical Study of Randomness* (Finishing Line Press, 2021). Kendra lives in Utah with her husband and poodle. When she's not writing, you can find her hiking, watching reality TV, or attempting to pet every animal she sees. You can find out more about her work at kendranuttall.com. Kendra joined *Capsule Stories* as a reader in January 2021.

Rachel Skelton, Reader

Rachel Skelton graduated from William Woods University with a BA in English, a concentration in writing, and a secondary major in business administration, a concentration in management. She has interned for Dzanc Books and now works as a freelance fiction editor specializing in speculative fiction. You can find more information about her work at theeditingskeleton.com. She occasionally tweets about editing at @EditingSkeleton and talks about books she's reading at @TheReadingSkeleton on Instagram. When she's not doing anything reading-related, she's hanging out with her cats, collecting houseplants, and attempting to learn how to crochet. Rachel joined *Capsule Stories* as a reader in January 2021.

Deanne Sleet, Reader

Deanne Sleet is a graduate of Saint Louis University with a BA in English, a concentration in creative writing, and minors in African American studies and women's and gender studies. She has interned for *River Styx* and Midwest Artist Project Services, where she gained experience with grant writing, editing, and writing copy. She is currently the leasing and marketing manager at City Lofts on Laclede and holds the secretary position for SLU's Black Alumni Association. She writes short fiction and poetry, and a novel is in the making. In her spare time, she hangs out with her cat and roller-skates. Deanne joined *Capsule Stories* as a reader in February 2021.

Claire Taylor, Reader

Claire Taylor is a writer in Baltimore, Maryland, where she lives with her husband, son, a bossy old cat, and an anxious dog who longs to be the cat's best friend. Claire's writing has appeared in a variety of publications, and she was a finalist for the 2020 Lascaux Prize in Poetry and winner of the 2021 *Serotonin* New Year's Day poetry competition. Her micro-chapbook, *A History of Rats*, is available from Ghost City Press. Claire is the founder and editor in chief of *Little Thoughts Press*, a print literary magazine of writing for and by kids. Claire joined *Capsule Stories* as a reader in March 2021. A selection of Claire's work is available online at clairemtaylor.com.

Submission Guidelines

Capsule Stories **is a print literary magazine** published once every season. Our first issue was published on March 1, 2019, and we accept submissions year-round.

Become published in a literary magazine run by like-minded people. We have a penchant for pretty words, an affinity to the melancholy, and an undeniably time-ful aura. We believe that stories exist in a specific moment, and that that moment is what makes those stories unique.

What we're really looking for are stories that can touch the heart. Stories that come from the heart. Stories about love, identity, the self, the world, the human condition. Stories that show what living in this world as the human you are is like.

We accept short stories, poems, and remarkably written essays. For short stories and essays, we're interested in pieces under 3,000 words. You may include up to five poems in a single poetry submission (please send them all in one Word document), and only send one story or essay at a time. Please send previously unpublished work only—a piece is considered published if it has been posted or made publicly available on a blog, website, or social media platform. You may only submit one submission per edition. Simultaneous submissions are okay, but please let us know if your submission is accepted elsewhere. Please include a brief third-person bio with your submission, and attach your submissions in a Word document (no PDFs unless your poetry has very specific formatting, please!).

Find our full submission guidelines and current theme descriptions at capsulestories.com/submissions.

Connect with us!
capsulestories.com
@CapsuleStories on Twitter and Facebook
@CapsuleStoriesMag on Instagram